A John Catt Publication

Playing
with Fire

Embracing Risk
and Danger
in Schools

By Mike Fairclough

"An educational manifesto for ~~~ times…"

~~~r Bill Lucas

First Published 2016

by John Catt Educational Ltd,
12 Deben Mill Business Centre, Old Maltings Approach,
Melton, Woodbridge IP12 1BL

Tel: +44 (0) 1394 389850 Fax: +44 (0) 1394 386893
Email: enquiries@johncatt.com
Website: www.johncatt.com

ISBN: 978 1 911382 072

Set and designed by John Catt Educational Limited
Back cover photograph by Russell Sach

"A man after my own heart, Mike Fairclough believes in the Jesuit principle of management – namely that it is easier to beg forgiveness than seek permission. In this down-to-earth book he energises readers to be creative risk-takers in the best interests of providing memorable and meaningful learning for primary children."
Roy Blatchford, Founding Director, National Education Trust

"This is a book about taking risks and embracing challenges. Mike Fairclough gives an inspirational account of what 'learning' can look like when you have a bronze age settlement and a herd of water buffalo at your school."
Sue Cowley, teacher, best-selling author

"A wonderful book. Mike Fairclough puts us all back in touch with essential parts of ourselves and our responsibilities as educators – to challenge, inspire and nurture in children a love of real life and the outdoors. It is essential reading for all teachers and school leaders, at any point in their careers."
William Stow, Head of the School of Teacher Education and Development, Canterbury Christ Church University

"Just like a visit to West Rise Junior School, Mike's book is refreshing, inspiring, warm, exciting, principled and massively thought-provoking. We need the balance, values and excitement that West Rise offers, in every school."
Jonathan Barnes, author of *Cross-Curricular Learning*

"Inspiring examples backed by sound educational principles coupled with straightforward advice makes this book the ideal launchpad for rethinking your school's approach to creative and risky endeavours.
Now, where are those matches?"
@ThatBoyCanTeach, Classroom-based Primary Academy senior leader

"Once in a while you encounter someone who inspires you. Hearing about and then meeting Mike Fairclough was one such encounter for me. I spent most of my tenure as Chair of HSE encouraging teachers and parents to recognise their role in helping children to learn about risk to prepare them for life. Here is someone who does exactly that and much, much more. Every school should own a copy of this book and learn from this teacher's shining example."
Dame Judith Hackitt DBE FREng former Chair of HSE

4

Contents

Foreword

Education in England is in a strange place today.

While there's much encouraging talk of the importance of 'growth mindsets' and 'grit' and character, there is also a deeply negative and fearful parallel conversation in too many staff rooms about Ofsted and EBacc and test worries.

Step forward Mike Fairclough, headteacher of West Rise Junior School with *Playing with Fire: Embracing risk and danger in schools*. The book is a brilliant and believably practical analysis of what schools can do if those who lead them have sufficient imagination and self-belief to ignore the unhelpful conversations which all too often swirl around us.

Playing with Fire is an educational manifesto for our times.

Why do I say this?

Let's start with the five aims discussed in the book, inspired by the work of Bedales School in Hampshire, and which I've edited very slightly here:

1. Develop independent thinkers with a love of learning who cherish independent thought.

This is a perfect combination of values (independence and lifelong learning) with evidence (as Nobel laureate James Heckman and others have shown), for cultivating these habits of mind has many practical benefits to children's life chances as well as helping them to better in all aspects of school and life!

2. Enable students to develop through doing and making.

Originally the three Rs were reading, wroughting and arithmetic. But in the 1850s wroughting (making or fashioning something as in a 'wheelwright') got dropped in favour of reading. The academic-practical divide was born. René

Descartes started all of this by suggesting that mind and body were separate and different in the sixteenth century. He was wrong. We now know that almost everything we do uses both mind and body working together in harmony behind the scenes. It's critically important that schools help children to see the value of hand and head work.

3. Foster individuality and encourage initiative, creativity and an appreciation of the beautiful.

Creativity is rightly being described as a vital literacy of our century. It encompasses individuality and initiative and many other attributes. To add a love of beauty to is an act of genius. While this attribute is an expression of a value (noticing beauty in the world really matters) there is powerful evidence of the importance of appreciating beauty to be derived from the work of Christopher Peterson and Martin Seligman.

4. Enable students, former students, parents and staff to take pride in and nourishment from the community's distinctiveness.

This is a powerful statement of so many things which we know help students thrive: parental engagement, pride and distinctiveness. The important emphasis on the locally distinctive puts me in mind of the work of the charity Common Ground. West Rise Junior makes a strong statement for both the local and, in the fifth aim, for the global.

5. Foster interest beyond the school, engaging with the local community and developing national and international awareness.

West Rise Junior has certainly got the interest of the local and national community! Its students have been blessed with a kind of education which defies national boundaries. Hooray!

But if you spend time with Mike then I suggest you may want to be careful about what you wish for. While many educationalists might agree with much of his vision, few would expect that it would be expressed through initiatives such as water buffalo running wild across 120 acres of marshland, and letting children do a range of impressively dangerous things from shooting to fire-making.

And that's just for starters. You'll have to read the book to gain a real understanding of what playing with fire means in his part of the South Downs.

In 1990 I was the founding director of a charity called Learning through Landscapes. We had a dream of transforming school grounds to make them places of wonder and sustainable ecology where children could learn by doing, caring and mistake-making. A shining example of this vision was and is Coombes Infant School where the inspirational Sue Humphries and Susan

Rowe turned an ordinary few acres into a wonderland with a mini Stonehenge, bird-hide, ponds galore and a classroom half way up a mature tree. These school leaders, like Mike Fairclough, were bold and brave. As a consequence schools can be places of beauty and challenge and excitement. Mike for me sits proudly in this tradition.

Last year, with my friend Guy Claxton, I wrote my own call to action, *Educating Ruby: What our children really need to learn.* In it we argue that schools have become polarized by silly binary choices: progressive versus traditional, academic versus practical, subject knowledge versus character or capability. We argued for seven Cs – confidence, curiosity, collaboration, communication, creativity, commitment and craftsmanship. I hadn't met Mike at this stage.

Now I have. Reading *Playing with Fire* I realise that the fictional Ruby of our book would be in heaven at his school.

This book is expansive in its conception of education of the desired outcomes of a child's school days. It is a serious corrective to a risk-adverse world, carefully explaining why it is possible to do potentially dangerous things in a character, values and skill-forming way. It takes learning out of the classroom into the real world where it belongs without compromising the necessary disciplinary progress that students need to make – West Rise is an outstanding school for both Ofsted and for someone with my values. It reconnects children to the natural world when too many of them have lost any link with the seed to seed cycle, with care for creatures and with the awe that landscapes like this can inspire. It is an awesome laboratory for the development of character and capability.

Above all *Playing with Fire* is, for me, about trust. Trust children to set up and run an art studio. Trust parents that they will let you take risks. Trust teachers to let go. Trust us all that we need help from those who understand animals and wetlands and archaeology if we are to be real lifelong learners. Trust your luck that when the water buffalo get out, the village will understand. Trust that there are great Ofsted inspectors who see through the ordinary. Trust that not all health and safety people are the problem. And trust that, fortified by this book, you can play with fire in your own backyard.

Professor Bill Lucas
Director, Centre for Real-World Learning at the University of Winchester

Dedicated to my father
Gordon Fairclough
1930-2016
Artist, Lover, Reveller, Gentleman

Introduction:
Embracing Risk and Danger

Many headteachers, teachers and parents ask me how it is that I can have a herd of water buffalo roaming around my school grounds and regularly take children shooting with shotguns. Why am I "allowed" to build a Bronze Age roundhouse with my pupils and teach them beekeeping and expose them to bee shamanism, amongst many other unconventional pursuits at my state-funded, mainstream junior school. They almost always ask me, "so how do you get away with it?"

There is a misconception, within the teaching profession, the media and the general public, that the Health and Safety Executive (HSE), the Government and Ofsted are all against the idea of children being exposed to danger. There is a misconception that schools are prevented from giving their children experiences which involve risk. The reality is that every school can take risks and engage in "dangerous" activities, in the same way that I have done so at my school for years. Furthermore, there are no individuals or organisations who are stopping them from doing so. The reality is that the Government, Ofsted and the HSE would all love to see schools embracing danger and in fact are encouraging them to do so.

This book is about risk-taking in schools, in the broadest sense, and is designed to empower headteachers, teachers, governors and parents, to provide activities for their pupils which include an element of risk and calculated danger. Woven into this is the subject of creativity and the arts, which I believe go hand in hand with this approach. It is essentially about educating the whole child by engaging in stimulating and enriching activities.

It is also about cultivating an ethos and attitude which are compatible with risk-taking and danger. The theme of building grit and resilience also runs throughout the book. These two traits are required in order for adults and children to fully embrace risk and danger.

The first chapter describes the context and recent history of West Rise Junior School and focuses primarily on the school's unique location. West Rise sits between an area of 120 acres of marshland, which the school manages, and the council estates from which most of the children derive. I will also touch on "Forest School" and encourage you to engage with your own school's outside environment.

This is followed by a chapter about "Room 13", a pupil-run art studio at West Rise. The ethos of which pervades the entire school and which I feel is very important to describe. It involves a different kind of risk taking and has the crucial ingredients of trust and creative freedom at its heart. Without a degree of trust and freedom, doing activities involving risk and danger is impossible.

I will then dispel some of the health and safety myths surrounding dangerous activities within schools, which are the main reason why school leaders tell me that they feel fearful about engaging in "dangerous" activities with their pupils. I will tell you why the Health and Safety Executive (HSE) actually want our children to have experiences which include risk and danger, within a carefully structured and well managed context. This information comes from working directly with the former Chair of the HSE during on a joint project in 2016 to attempt to wake schools up to the truth about health and safety. This is followed by a discussion about Ofsted. Ofsted is also unfairly blamed for schools not being allowed to take risks, or to be creative and I will show that the opposite is true. I hope that this information will empower headteachers, teachers and parents to feel more positive and confident about doing the things that they believe in.

I will discuss the philosophy behind my approach and why I believe that schools need to provide children with rich, hands-on educational experiences that involve risk and danger. We will explore how moving children out of their comfort zones builds character, resilience and trust. I will explain why these are important traits to cultivate, if we are to help children face life's challenges and to give them the strength to succeed in the face of adversity. Similarly, I will discuss how I believe that school leaders and teachers also need to move out of their comfort zones and to become examples of the change that they wish to see within the education system. The main obstacle between schools wishing that they could be doing amazing things and actually doing them are their limiting beliefs and fears of failure. I want to expose this and offer ways to move into a new, more positive way of thinking, so that schools feel confident about embracing the things they have always longed to be able to do. I will also explain how enhancing natural chemicals within the body may assist us on this journey.

Chapter Five explores another imagined barrier which many professionals say gets in the way of children working outside and being creative. I will show how video gaming can be used as a hook to inspire children to engage in the physical world and also hope to show that the virtual world can actually assist children's progress within physical reality. Like health and safety, I believe that video gaming is misrepresented and not understood deeply enough within the teaching profession. I will aim to show an alternative view which may surprise the reader and show how the hobby can be a hook and inspiration for activities involving risk and danger.

Offering another example of inspiring work, this time within the independent school sector, I will go on to describe a few examples of risk-taking and creativity at Bedales School in Hampshire and the philosophy behind their approach. Bedales has a similar culture to West Rise and has developed a framework and ideology within which to educate children in this hands-on way. It shows that educators have been working in this way for decades.

I will show what the academic impact of working outside and having real and memorable experiences has on the children at my school. I will also touch on the spiritual and emotional impact.

A chapter is dedicated to the practical "how to" side of preparing for and implementing risky activities. It is very simple and will give headteachers and teachers all the tools they need in order to embark on exciting activities with their children involving an element of risk.

Woven into the book are examples of my work at West Rise Junior School in Eastbourne, where I have been the headteacher for 12 years. This includes stories about beekeeping, water buffalo breeding, shooting, archery, Forest School, paddle boarding and skinning rabbits which are amongst many other unusual pursuits. There are some interesting anecdotes attached to many of these examples and I hope that you will enjoy them. They are told to show the reader how teething problems and mistakes are part and parcel of this approach to education and should be embraced.

I have also written some "Ideas for Teachers" which are suggested in order to help you apply this approach within your own school and practice immediately. You will have lots of ideas of your own and may already be working in this way, nonetheless I hope to offer a bit of inspiration.

Ultimately, the purpose of this book is to remove the "cotton wool culture" which the teaching profession, the media and the public have unfairly accused the authorities of wrapping around our children. I offer a holistic approach to replace our fears about doing risky and dangerous activities with our children and invite schools to tear off the cotton wool from around our kids and cast it into the flames. We can do what we want right now. We have full permission to play with fire.

Chapter 1

Ancient Land Revived

I would like to begin by describing the context of West Rise Junior School and its location. This will give the reader a big picture and a short history of the school and will introduce you to some of the activities which we engage in on a daily basis.

West Rise Junior School, where I am the headteacher, is a state-funded school for boys and girls between the ages of seven and eleven. The 274 children derive primarily from the two local council estates, Shinewater and Langney in Eastbourne. The school is about a mile away from the beach and is overlooked by a range of weathered and majestic hills, known as the South Downs.

The school is subject to the same Government guidance and regulations as any other maintained school in England. We carry out national statutory tests, or SATs and are inspected by the UK Inspectorate, Ofsted, on a regular basis.

When I first meet people and tell them what I do, they often ask me whether West Rise is an independent school on account of the range of activities we offer our children. It is important to emphasise that West Rise is not an independent school and is a "normal" school within the context of mainstream education. People will then assume that the school is exclusively populated by middle class kids and that our positive test results and good Ofsted reports are a foregone conclusion – "surely that's why you can get away with what you do?" The reality is that the school is largely made up of children from areas of social and economic deprivation. Two thirds of our children are, or have been, eligible for Free School Meals within the last six years, which is the Department for Education's main deprivation indicator and is well above the national average.

As for the positive test results and Ofsted reports, they are the product of hard work and aspirational thinking on the part of the entire school community. They are also the product of our approach to risk-taking. We get the results because of our innovations and not in spite of them.

However, it our location, within its historical and geographical context, which has shaped us into what has become a distinctly "unusual" place for teaching and learning.

The Bronze Age

The school is located on land where the second largest Bronze Age settlement in Europe was once situated. The Late Bronze Age, some 3000 years ago, was a melting pot of ideas, cultures, technology and the arts for the region. Due to its geographical situation, next to the sea and surrounded by lush and fertile land, the site became internationally significant. There was a vibrant trading culture between the people living there and the rest of Europe, from as far afield as the Baltics and beyond. Many of the artefacts which have been discovered by archaeologists under the ground on this site are so significant and rare that they are now on display at the British Museum in London.

Being on a major archaeological site is an exciting educational opportunity and at West Rise we have embraced the Bronze Age and integrated the energy of it into our curriculum in many ways.

I originally learned about the prehistoric significance of the school site from the man who first discovered it back in 1995, an archaeologist called Chris Greatorex. I visited Chris with Alex Richards, who is now my school Farm Manager, and was blown away by what he told us. Chris is a real life Indiana Jones, who discovered the Bronze Age site whilst walking his dog around the area when a new housing development was underway. Construction diggers had dug deep into the marshy ground and taken off thick layers of black peat. They were excavating the area to build what was to become Shinewater Estate. The activity of the machines had exposed, for the first time in thousands of years, numerous upright wooden stakes, which Chris instantly recognised as being of prehistoric origin and part of some kind of massive structure.

Chris told us this story whilst Alex and I listened with increasing interest and excitement. Standing in one of the rooms of his house, he then crouched down next to a cabinet and pulled out an array of fascinating artefacts. "No one is doing anything with this stuff," Chris told us. "The local authority and schools don't seem very interested at the moment." The artefacts included bones, which he had personally excavated from the site, bronze axe heads and fragments of unusual looking pottery. He then revealed a perfectly preserved 3,000-year-old oak wooden stake. "You can borrow this if you like," said Chris with a wide grin and from that point on Alex and I were completely hooked!

I was driving around in a 1970s VW camper van at the time, which had to be pushed to get it started. Alex and I loaded up the van with all of the artefacts Chris had given us. We then pushed the vehicle down the road, jumped in and returned to school, feeling absolutely awesome. This was the start of our Bronze Age project.

Three thousand years ago the Bronze Age landscape in Eastbourne was one of marshes and small rivulets leading out to the sea. The marshes would have been teaming with life, from fish to wild fowl, and would have made excellent hunting grounds. The area would have been covered in reeds and bulrushes, waterlogged in the winter and dryer in the warmer months. Fortuitously for us, this is exactly what the landscape is like adjacent to the main school grounds. Although the school is situated on a built up council estate, it is also on the edge of a large wetland habitat, overlooked by the cinematic range of chalky hills which rise up from the sea and surrounding area. Along the entire crest of the hills are about fifty ancient burial mounds. These predate the Bronze Age settlement, but would have been an important ancestral element of the sacred landscape nonetheless.

Soon after acquiring the artefacts, Alex heard on the grapevine that the grazing license on the marshland, opposite the school, was due for renewal. So, nine years ago, after hearing about the Bronze Age settlement from Chris, we approached the Local Authority to ask if we could lease the entire 120 acres of grazing land, plus two large lakes. We wanted the area to be the environment for a living history project exploring the Bronze Age and also had an idea that we could run our own farm with the children from the school. After discussion, the Local Authority generously agreed a 10 year grazing tenancy for £900 a year and were only too happy to support the school with its project.

Just as it would have been in prehistoric times, the site is heaving with wildlife, which it is important to protect and manage. After some research, I applied for funding to support the wildlife on the site and managed to secure annual funding from Natural England for us to maintain the area. Natural England carried out an assessment of the habitat and found it to have a huge abundance of fauna and flora deserving of conservation. They also described it as the last truly wild space of natural beauty left in the town before reaching the South Downs. This enabled us to access further funding, which we used to buy a tractor and a quad bike as well as a small flock of sheep.

We kept the Local Authority informed about our endeavours and also began to engage with local councillors and the local media to gain support and enthusiasm for our vision. This was the first time I seriously began to engage with the media and to see how important it is to have their support.

It is fair to say at this point that we were learning as we were going along. Neither Alex nor I had any background in farming, although I had grown up in the countryside. However, we were extremely enthusiastic and welcomed the advice from Natural England. Alex was also able to receive guidance from local farmers who were friends and supporters of the school. I have personally found that I learn things more quickly by actually doing them, which is something that has become quite integral to our approach to teaching and learning with the children at the school.

Obtaining the lease on the land was just the beginning of a project which would soon become the hub of the school and which would provide all of the children and teachers with some extraordinary and unique experiences. It was around this time and after farming our sheep for about a year, that we began to share our new environment with some extremely unusual school pets, a herd of Asian water buffalo.

The water buffalo

Doing new and innovative things occasionally rubs people up the wrong way, especially when mistakes are made. Unfortunately for me, I had already made quite a significant mistake and was now under investigation by Trading Standards for the suspected "Illegal movement of livestock". Perhaps a little naively, Alex and I thought that once our sheep had gone off to slaughter, that we could freely sell the meat to the parents of our pupils. Apparently not.

An imposingly tall Trading Standards Officer visited me at the school after informing me over the phone that there was some essential paperwork missing from our records. I was therefore in breach of the law. My office staff were convinced that I would be led off in hand cuffs at the very least for this oversight. I remember them finding it very amusing that I was sweating it out and racking my brains trying to think of a good excuse for my error. When he arrived, Alex and I sat in my office and looked on in silence at the officer. "You can't just kill your sheep and sell them without filling out the paperwork," he told us. "There are laws which you must follow." He spoke and we nodded.

However, far from being carted off to jail, as my office staff had predicted, the officer said that he would help us get our paperwork in order and then, leaning forward and with a completely different expression, said "I love what you're doing! Have you thought about lambing?" I wasn't exactly sure that I had heard him correctly, but before I could fully analyse the situation, he then said "and would you like a herd of water buffalo?"

The Trading Standards Officer told us that there was a herd for sale a few miles up the road in the South Downs, in a village called Firle. There we would meet a passionate farmer who would either "love you or kick you off his land". There we would discover that the farmer was selling aspects of his vast menagerie. This included an ostrich, some exotic looking pigs and a large number of buffalo, amongst many other animals. I think Alex and I felt a mixture of huge relief, as well as disbelief, about this turn of events. However, the main feelings were of overwhelming euphoria and boyish excitement at the prospect of obtaining these extravagant beasts.

You can imagine my office staff's surprise and disappointment when I walked out of the office with a huge smile on my face and announced "We're getting a herd of water buffalo!"

The next day Alex and I visited the farm and hit it off nicely with the farmer. He sold us seven of his water buffalo for a total of £700. The day after that we collected them in a huge trailer and brought them back to school.

Our continuing research into the Bronze Age revealed that 3,000 years ago, massive horned cattle called "aurochs" roamed our local marshes. A happy coincidence is that water buffalo are the closest living relatives to the now extinct auroch. They are also perfect for grazing wetland habitats due to their wide feet and love of water. Our Natural England agreement states that we must graze the land in order to maintain it, so this was ideal.

Alex promptly became the new Farm Manager and used his contacts within the local farming fraternity to learn everything he could, from lookering to fencing, in order to carry out his new role.

Over the next few months, we taught the children to look after the buffalo in addition to other animals we had acquired over the past year. The water buffalo herd is now well established on the marsh and we have even become successful water buffalo breeders, with one or two babies born every couple of years.

An evolving project

Further research into the Bronze Age showed that our ancestors navigated the dykes and rivers in the area in oval-shaped boats called coracles. In perfect synchronicity, our school adviser at the time had three coracles in her garage which her husband, a history enthusiast, had built some years previously. I find it amazing that when a person is tuned into a particular thought or idea, that life will present opportunities and chance meetings which are compatible with those thoughts or ideas. It might be that we are subconsciously looking for those connections, but whatever it is, it is a fantastic phenomenon when it comes to creative projects. We collected the vessels from our friendly advisor and started to teach the children at the school to row them on our lakes. Whilst we were at it, Alex also showed the children how to fish with reed rods and goose feather quills collected from the marsh. Our living history project was beginning to evolve and take shape.

Each time we embarked on a significant new innovation, I would contact the local press and invite local dignitaries to the school in order to endorse the projects.

With the land, animals and boats in place, we began work on building a Bronze Age village on our marsh. One summer, Year 6 pupils, aged between ten and eleven, spent several days working with our site managers to construct an 80-metre long, raised wooden causeway across the wetland. This was a replica of one of the preserved finds discovered during the earlier archaeological excavation of the site. The original was an eight-metre wide, half-mile long, raised wooden causeway with an east-west alignment. In the late Bronze Age and in one season, the ancestors living in Eastbourne chopped down hundreds of mature oak trees on the edge of the South Downs. They then crafted the trees into large stakes using deer antlers and flint axe heads. An astonishing feat of craftsmanship and engineering, which is mind boggling to comprehend for people in our modern age. The replica wooden causeway, built by the children at West Rise, joins a large wooden platform. The platform rises up from one of our lakes, on which is built a Bronze Age replica roundhouse. In ancient times, the ancestors would have lived in structures elevated above the flood plain on stilts, which is what this structure was designed to reflect. Again, the children were involved in all aspects of the construction, including the thatching of the roof. This was carried out by our Year 5 pupils aged between eight and nine years. Alex and our other site manager, Paul Hemmings, worked tirelessly on this project and engaged the children at every step of the way. Giving children hands-on experiences like this gives them a real taste of what it might have been like for their ancestors, splinters and all. The children got muddy and bruised, working hard until the construction was complete.

Since creating our Bronze Age habitat on the marsh, we have worked alongside Eastbourne Museum and continue to work with Chris Greatorex. These experts teach our students about a wide range of Prehistoric crafts. Using the fleece from our flock of sheep, the children learn to spin and dye wool. The dye is made from plants and berries, depending on the time of year, and are collected from the marsh. The dyes are then prepared using traditional methods. The children also excavate clay from the marsh and make replica Bronze Age pots, firing them over an open fire. Eastbourne Museum lend us artefacts from the archaeological excavations on the marsh, including fragments of clay pots which the children are allowed to handle and examine. Some of these fragments have the finger prints of their original prehistoric makers indented into the clay. You can imagine how powerful it is when a child puts their fingers into the indentations made by their ancestors. Out on the marsh, in the roundhouse, with the water buffalo roaming around like great aurochs, the children are able to experience true time travel. It feels as if they are in communication with their ancestors in ways which can never be replicated in the classroom. We also teach the children a range of traditional open-fire cooking techniques and have even had them skinning rabbits and plucking pigeons with Alex.

One of the most inspiring activities we have carried out with every child within the school, on a number of occasions too, is smelting tin and copper to make bronze. Under the supervision of a trained practitioner, the children use bellows to raise the temperature of an earth furnace to 1000 degrees. They then drop the tin and copper into a crucible and witness the alchemical process of the two metals merging to become bronze. The children then pour the molten metal into sand moulds to make pendants and arrow heads. This is a technique which would have been used during the Bronze Age by people considered to have magical powers and of great status within the community. The Bronze Age was a time when our ancestors would have been evolving their technology from stone tools through to the more durable and adaptable bronze. A technology which would go on to change the entire world.

The curriculum

You might be wondering how this sort of thing can be "allowed" to take place within a mainstream school. I will talk about health and safety permission later on but would first like to address the requirements of the National Curriculum. The primary school curriculum is very broad indeed. At times, it is teachers and leaders who think too narrowly about the curriculum in my view. We need to think about themes which can span across subjects, thus approaching subject matters in different and more engaging ways in order to make the curriculum more compelling for pupils.

The Key Stage 2 history curriculum, for seven to 11-year-olds, spans in chronological order from the Stone Age through to 1066. It covers the Romans, Vikings, various histories of the ancient world and the option of a pivotal moment in British History. As long as the children learn the knowledge and skills within the curriculum and can demonstrate their understanding, there is no prescriptive way in which the profession is expected to deliver it. This can open up limitless possibilities for creative teaching and learning.

I have already described activities through our Bronze Age project which link to living things within science, habitats and within the geography curriculum. The theme also facilitates the teaching of aspects of art and design technology. All of the activities which the children enjoy within our Bronze Age project cover numerous aspects of the curriculum. Most importantly, their experiences are memorable and therefore the learning goes in deeply. The emotional connection that the children have with the experiences and the subject matter ensure that the skills and knowledge last.

I have been told by our local historians and archaeologists that the average age of a person in the Bronze Age was 14, with an average life expectancy of 26. This is important when you think about the achievements of this age; the elaborate crafts, the ingenuity, architecture in the form of stone buildings and the sophisticated social structures. If the average age was 14, then people of that age were the movers and shakers of the time. They were the inventors, travellers and master craftspeople. This is important to note as a key theme within this book.

Children and young people are much more capable than we realise or allow them to be and the curriculum can be the vehicle through which they can show us their talents.

Forest School

The Bronze Age has inspired many other projects at West Rise. One of the most influential projects has been the development of a weekly Forest School on the marsh. This has become an integral part of the provision and of each child's experience whilst attending the school.

Forest School is a hugely exciting project which is led by both Helen Stringfellow, a teacher at the school, and Paul, the school's site manager. Helen and Paul are assisted by a team of experienced parent helpers and other volunteers on a weekly basis. Thirty to 40 children are selected over the six terms of the year, enabling every child in the school to take part in the project throughout the year.

The Forest Schools Programme, which has training opportunities across the country, aims to provide a variety of stimulating, hands-on activities. The activities allow the children to take managed risks and to use tools which they would not normally have access to. At West Rise, our Forest School offers a wide range of activities and experiences for the children to engage in which often incorporate a topic-related focus, such as the Bronze Age. It is important to also note that the requirements of Personal Social Health Citizenship Education (PSHE) can all be met through Forest School as well as assisting children's Social, Moral, Spiritual, and Cultural development (SMSC). All of these are key aspects of the National Curriculum and will be looked on very favourably by Ofsted.

The creative ethos of Forest School is based on developing self-esteem, confidence, independence and responsibility in children of all ages and ability. It is achieved through hands-on and outdoor experiences within the natural environment, using tools and natural resources.

It teaches children to safely evaluate risks for themselves and to responsibly engage in new activities. Self-motivation, independence, teamwork and problem solving are all fostered through this approach.

How it works

Three times a week, adults and children from the school will get dressed into waterproof clothing, gather bundles of wood, tea kettles, tarpaulin and other equipment. They then make the ten-minute trek from the main school site, across to the marsh, regardless of the weather. Once on location, close to the Bronze Age Roundhouse, they learn new skills and develop existing ones, including the use of various tools, such as bow saws and axes. They also learn green woodworking skills. The children will all make disks from green wood on which they write messages and make charcoal pencils from elder wood.

Every child will also learn how to lay and light fires. They use fire to make charcoal, boil water to cook with and to make drinks. Children will also plant willow whips for future green woodworking resources, as well as take part in activities such as bird watching and identification with members of the local RSPB. Every child will also learn medicinal herb gathering to prepare tinctures of various kinds alongside a trained practitioner.

The school marsh, with our herd of water buffalo, farm activities and Bronze Age construction, is the environment for learning. Nevertheless, it is the regularity and consistency of Forest School, which has given the project greater depth over time. This is due to the spirit of Forest School and to the wide ranging variety of skills which the children learn during their time at West Rise.

Examples of activities the children will experience at Forest School

- Fire building and lighting. Campfire cooking
- Making hot drinks with a Kelly Kettle
- Shelter building

- Making clay pots
- Bird watching and identification
- Pond dipping
- Trust/team building games
- Ecology games
- Nature identification and conservation
- Making wooden name tags
- Making wooden mallets
- Making tent pegs
- Making charcoal pencils

Examples of tools used at Forest School

- Fire steels
- Bowsaw
- Secateurs
- Loppers
- Peelers
- Knife
- Drills
- Kelly Kettle

Ideas for Teachers

In this chapter, I have talked about the location of West Rise Junior School as the inspiration for how we approach the curriculum. The first thing I encourage other headteachers and teachers to do is to look for the learning opportunities within your own immediate environment. What outside spaces do you have? What is the local history of the area? Are there any significant geographical features?

If you have little outside space, this is not a problem at all. Even if you only have a tarmac playground, you can still deliver a vibrant Forest School and other outdoor learning opportunities within a small area.

A controlled fire only takes up a small amount of space. You do not need 120 acres of marshland to teach children how to light and cook over an open fire. I have made fires in very small areas and successfully worked with children to cook flat bread and boil a kettle, whilst also teaching them green woodworking skills.

If you are limited with space, I would recommend creating a permanent fire pit, dug into the ground and surrounded by lengths of wood to form a boundary. If this is on the grass playing field, as we have had to do when the marsh has been flooded and inaccessible, the turf can be replaced at the end of the session and it will not damage the field in any way. Round logs for sitting on can be obtained from tree surgeons and from areas of woodland management. Even if your school is in the heart of the city, it is possible to order wood or travel out to pick it up yourself.

Whatever you have in terms of local history and geography, this can become the hub of your curriculum and the environment in which exciting learning takes place. Of course It does not have to be of Prehistoric origin. Fire building can be linked to the Victorians and World War Two themes, as well as earlier periods in history. Remember also that working outside links to the PSHE curriculum and to SMSC development, as previously mentioned. The idea is to make as many cross curricular connections as you can.

Even if you do not wish to start with fire making, engaging with your local museum and with local historians and archaeologists will open up doors and help you to make links to the National Curriculum. This will lead to practical, hands-on activities that you can do with your children. This is how many of the activities we have introduced at West Rise first began. Rather than starting with a blank canvas, or with little knowledge, an expert in the field will be able to generate plenty of ideas.

I would like to emphasise that you do not need to have a definitive long term vision when you first start working in this way. Your project will evolve organically over time in an intuitive fashion. Once you have lit that first spark, the rest will follow. New people will be attracted to your school or organisation once you have begun and you will learn new skills and knowledge as you proceed.

Look at the Forest School Association website (www.forestschoolassociation. org) and see where your nearest training centre is. Forest School training is very comprehensive and will enable you to embark on many of the activities which we enjoy at West Rise.

As for keeping animals, the best ones to start with are chickens. It is essential that you have someone who can look after them on a daily basis, but maintaining the area in which they live and feeding them is very easy to do. Once you have set up a chicken coop for a couple of hens, the children can be taught to feed them and to collect the eggs. It all starts from there.

Chapter 2

Room 13

Although not a risk to life and limb, Room 13 has had a powerful and lasting effect on the culture of my school. The idea of Room 13 is challenging to many teachers and schools, some of which are still rooted in control ideologies of the past. However, the essence of the project underpins all of the activities which involve children being exposed to risk and danger at my school.

The philosophy of Room 13 promotes the same philosophy of trust, freedom and autonomy found within our Forest School provision. It is an ethos which is invaluable when it comes to risk-taking. Room 13 and Forest School collaborate on frequent projects at West Rise and I believe that it is the spirit of Room 13 which has enabled us as a school to embrace risk and danger in such a big way.

Background to Room 13

Room 13 was first conceived in 1994 by a group of pupils at Caol Primary School in Fort William, Scotland. The children had been working with a local artist on an art project, which had been funded by the school. When the project came to an end, the children wanted to continue working with the artist and asked their headteacher whether this would be possible. The headteacher said that the only way that this could happen would be if the children themselves paid for the artist's time and materials. She also said they would need to use a spare classroom, which was not being used by anyone else. The children approached the artist who agreed to the idea and together they set up an art studio in one of the school's spare classrooms. This particular room in the school was called "Room 13".

Due to the fact that the children, all between the ages of seven and eleven, had been given the responsibility of running the project, the first thing they did was to set up a "management team". The team comprised of a managing director, chairman, treasurer, site managers and communication officer. They opened up their own bank account and started to apply for funding. The artist worked in the studio on his own work and the children worked alongside him. He would advise the children when they needed help and in turn, he would be inspired by their work.

This all happened because Caol's headteacher gave her children free reign to run with their idea. She firmly believed that children can do amazing things, beyond the limited beliefs of adults, if they are given the opportunity. It was also the heart-centred vision and support of the artist in residence, Rob Fairley, who empowered the children to really take ownership of the project.

The children were enormously resourceful, ambitious and successful. Soon Room 13 became a thriving business. They bought equipment, set up exhibitions, took commissions, sold artwork and began to make a profit. Catriona Jackson, an eleven-year-old, who was managing director of Room 13 at the time, applied to the Scottish Arts Council for a grant of £19,000, which she managed to secure. The children employed a further artist, Wendy Sutherland, and soon private companies were beginning to support Room 13. They also received funding from Enterprise Scotland.

In 2002 the children won £20,000 for the Barbie Prize for the quality of their artwork. The Barbie Prize is considered to be the junior Turner Prize by many within the art world. The treasurer wanted to give all of the money to the artists, but the management team decided that instead it should be used to benefit the entire school. They bought a reserve of materials and used part of the money to pay for the artists' time. After this success, two girls on the committee filled out a fourteen-page application form for funding from NESTA. The committee exchanged emails and telephone calls between London and Scotland for several months and were eventually awarded £200,000 to fund their project. This was another tremendous achievement on the part of the children and a further example of what children are capable of if given the opportunity.

Room 13 became very well-known and the artwork generated achieved critical acclaim in Scotland and England. Thanks to the grant, the model began to be replicated in other schools and, in 2004, Channel 4 aired a documentary about the project.

I don't think that most adults would believe that children could be capable of such an achievement, but this is exactly what happened. My observation is that children do not have the same limiting beliefs and cynicism that adults sometimes build up over the years. There are numerous stories of children being told that they can't do certain things by adults only to prove the adults wrong further down the line. A recent example of this is the British gymnast, Max Whitlock, who was told when he was younger that he had "the wrong feet to be a gymnast" only to go on to win two gold medals in gymnastics during the 2016 Olympics. Remember also what I said about the capabilities of people 3000 years ago in the Bronze Age and the fact that the vast majority of them were teenagers. It would appear that as a culture we sometimes limit and restrict our children when they could be capable of achieving very much more.

Room 13 at West Rise

When I became headteacher of West Rise Junior School in 2004, I decided that I wanted to start a Room 13 after watching the Channel 4 programme about the project. Prior to doing my teacher training, I had spent five years being an art student in London where I studied painting, drawing and sculpture. I feel that I am an artist at heart and that my school is my creativity, so Room 13 seemed irresistible to me. I also believe in the limitless potential and positive energy of children and feel that they deserve to be given the opportunity to exceed our expectations.

Room 13 is run on the principles of creative freedom, autonomy and trust. Children can come out of class whenever they like, to create films, animations, paintings, sculptures or whatever they wish. The pupils simply have to stay up to date with their classwork and finish off tasks in their own time. Some teachers operate a rota system for children to engage with the project because it is so popular. In this way, teachers try to enable everyone who wishes to access the provision within their class to do so.

Introducing the concept of Room 13 to my new school, which at the time had more conventional principles and practices, was a challenge. It was not that I personally struggled with the idea, but for some staff, governors and parents it presented a massive culture change. I was able to access funding with the help of the Arts Council, which paid for flights and train fares for ten of our children and their parents, some governors, teachers and myself to visit Scotland. We felt that if we could see Room 13 in practice then we would be able to convince the school community that it works and to adopt the idea. We needed to find out how the philosophy of creative freedom and trust could work within an education system that is broadly based on control and boundaries.

When we visited Scotland, the basic message from the headteacher of Caol Primary School was simply to allow the pupils the freedom to get on with it. The artist in residence said that his role was to be creative and to encourage creativity in the children without controlling or judging how they express themselves. The children, who by now had evolved the management team model and had a long track record of creative success, were mind-blowing in their maturity and ability to organise themselves. They were shining examples of innovation and unlimited self-belief. I have met some of the committee members, years later as adults, and they are all thriving artists with very open minds.

The principles of Room 13 are so simple that we probably did not need to travel to Scotland to see it, however the adventure paid off in that it showed my commitment to developing our own Room 13 to the West Rise school community.

I have always believed that if a person believes in something strongly enough and acknowledges that anything is possible then they can achieve whatever they wish. This is how I felt about Room 13 and I could not wait to launch it at West Rise. I was relishing the opportunity to see where my pupils would take the concept and how it would influence the entire school.

In 2006, I converted the disused caretaker's house on the school site into a fully functioning art studio on two floors and presented the idea of Room 13 to my staff. The staff were split about the idea; many of them were still entrenched in the old style of teaching, where children are given a limited task and then expected to execute the task perfectly within the boundaries of the brief. Members of staff moved on to new schools which were more compatible with their way of thinking and others joined us who were more aligned with the new vision. Fortunately, from a recruitment point of view, the East Sussex coast is a hub of creativity and forward-thinking people. West Rise is close to Brighton, Lewes and Hastings which are all bohemian locations so it was not difficult to attract creative teachers to my school.

Several years on, the West Rise Room 13 is still flourishing. We have had five committees over the years and numerous exhibitions, publications and events. Children have created magnificent artwork, developed their creative autonomy and expanded their minds as well as the minds of the adults. Working alongside reputable artists in residence, the children and many of the adults consider Room 13 to be the creative hub of the school

An ethos which supports risk and danger

The creative ethos and energy of Room 13 has influenced every aspect of West Rise. It has shown me that children can be trusted and can do amazing things when they are shown trust and given freedom by the adults around them. All that teachers are required to do is to embrace the spirit of Room 13 and to believe in it.

The essence of Room 13 and its impact on the wider school has been far reaching and profound. Due to the responsibility which children inevitably take on, behaviour issues are very rare within the school and never occur in Room 13. The trust which pervades the school allows our children to be trusted to use knives and guns on the marsh in a mature and responsible manner. The children embrace the freedom which has been given to them, in turn this creates a relaxed and happy atmosphere throughout the whole school. The creative thinking associated with the project lends itself perfectly to the sort of enquiry which children engage in when out on the marsh. Activities such as foraging for medicinal herbs or stumbling across the remains of a dead animal always lead on to some sort of investigation.

Room 13 and Forest School collaborate frequently, because visual art and nature go hand in hand at the school. An example of this is the "shelf of death" on the ground floor of the studio. The ground floor is also the resources base for Forest School. Here the children put the skulls and vertebra which they have collected from the marsh. These will later be sent upstairs to Room 13 where the children will examine and draw them. Recently, a child found the remains of an adder which was the first to be discovered on the marsh. The adder has become the subject matter of lots of artwork and even inspired stories and songs.

The important thing to emphasise is that I am not dictating that every child across the country needs to pick up a shotgun and start firing it, or that lighting fires for the sake of it will benefit every school. It goes much deeper than that to a level which is enshrined within the values of Room 13. It is about creating a culture which is compatible with giving children freedom and one where teachers are more open-minded and relaxed.

This is not about being complacent and leaving it all up to the kids. There is a huge amount of planning and organisation which underpins every project that we deliver at West Rise. Once the structure is in place and everyone knows what they are doing, the culture of creative freedom and trust allow for endless possibilities.

Rob Fairly contacted me recently after following the recent developments of the school in the national press. He has been an avid supporter of the school for years and given us continued support since we first established our own Room 13. He said that West Rise is possibly the only true Room 13 left in the British Isles, with regards to creative freedom. He told me that others have fallen by the wayside due to changes of management within schools and the changing climate in education. I want to urge all schools and school leaders to embrace the philosophy of Room 13 and to see that it is entirely compatible with the latest curriculum developments. Every school can have a Room 13 if it wishes to and still fulfil the requirements of the National Curriculum. Most importantly, the quality of trust and freedom are integral to the success of embarking on activities which involve an element of risk and danger. Room 13 is a fantastic way to grow a culture of trust and freedom within your own school setting and I urge all schools to at least consider adopting the idea.

Ideas for Teachers

Give more opportunities to your children to make decisions for themselves. At first, if they are not used to this, they will struggle and you may feel disheartened but that is simply because they are new to this way of working. Start small and then grow.

Access the support of local artists and parents who are willing to give their time to the school and to the children to share their expertise. The idea of Room 13 is that children work alongside an artist whilst being inspired by them; artists will similarly be inspired by the children in return. One of our current artist-in-residence is Ed Boxall who is an author, singer-songwriter and visual artist. Many of his personal projects have been directly inspired by working with the children. The project is so successful that he has been able to offer further Room 13's to other local schools. Artists also think differently to most classroom teachers and will make suggestions which will challenge you in positive ways.

You may also have creative and artistic people amongst your staff. At West Rise, Karen Stephens, who is a Higher Level Teaching Assistant, is also an artist-in-residence at the school. She has developed her skills across a wide range of media, including painting and photography, as a direct result of the Room 13 provision. She is also at the school five days a week allowing the project and the committee to continuously receive her support.

Engage with local galleries who will have artworks which you may be able to borrow. They may also have outreach programmes for your school to engage in.

Visit the Room 13 at West Rise; we flew all the way to Scotland from the South Coast of England before embarking on this project, so it is worth investing some time in seeing how it can be done. If not our studio, then visit one closer to your home.

Keep a sketch book yourself and fill it with your ideas, inspirations and aspirations. Cut out images from magazines and images printed from the internet which inspire you. This serves two purposes. One is that you will begin to start thinking like an artist and the second is that you will begin to play around with ideas which will in time become reality. Every one of my projects began with a mind map or picture, which I had drawn, before they physically manifested in the real world.

Chapter 3

'The System' is Not the Problem

This chapter places the responsibility of giving children amazing experiences completely in the hands of the professionals and parents who are looking after them. No more nonsense about children not being able to play with conkers or throw snowballs. No more blaming "The System" for not allowing us to do dangerous things. These beliefs are the result of myths generated by the media which are perpetuated by the education system and the general public. Wanting someone to blame for children no longer having the kind of childhood that we once had whilst also not really wanting to do anything about it, we have allowed these myths to become our reality. That can all change right now and with full permission from the authorities.

Health and safety myths

The Health and Safety Executive (HSE) is the national independent watchdog for work-related health, safety and illnesses. It has the power to close down an organisation, such as a school or business, if it feels that it is presenting a serious risk with regards to injury or death. The Health and Safety Executive is there because it is acting in the public interest to reduce work-related death and serious injury. The impact of its work is that there are now less work-related deaths and injuries than ever before. The law now holds those at the top of organisations to account in ensuring that their employees and others accessing their premises or work areas are kept safe. I personally can't see anything wrong with this approach at all, especially if the number of deaths and serious injuries are going down year on year. It means that people's lives, and the lives of their families, are not being destroyed by unnecessary tragedies or negligence.

On a recent health and safety course which I attended, the HSE were described as being "one step down from God" as they possess the power to walk in to any school and close it down if they find reason to do so. They provide guidance for schools and businesses and are extremely important when considering any activity which involves an element of risk and danger within a school. I strongly urge school leaders to engage with the HSE for advice and support, although very few people actually do this. Their website www.hse.gov.uk is full of guidance and policies and is the best first port of call.

It is an unfortunate fact that the HSE are also the ones who the media and the general public usually point their finger at when finding someone to blame for the "cotton wool culture" surrounding children and schools. The truth is that this is wholly inaccurate. The HSE want us to take risks but they want us to take them responsibly, with health and safety at the forefront of our minds.

A background on my work with the HSE

In June 2015, West Rise Junior School was named "*Times Educational Supplement* Primary School of the Year". A panel of judges in London, including prominent educationalists and people from the British media, looked at a shortlist of schools for this prestigious award and were asked, "Which school would you most like to teach in and which school would you send your children to?" The answer unanimously was "West Rise Junior School".

The news of the award came to me as my wife and I were hauling bails of straw off the back of a trailer and onto a friend's farm. We were setting up a Woodstock-style festival on the land for our wedding the following day. Already feeling absolutely great about getting married, my wife and I were delighted to hear the news that the school would receive such recognition. I had asked my senior managers to attend the award ceremony in London, in the hope that we might win, but I could not attend myself due to the work I needed to complete out on the land. My wife, Sundeep, who is a beautiful Punjabi-Indian with a Sikh warrior's strength and agility, was pitching in with the physical labour as much as I was and we were having lots of fun. I was more than happy to be hanging out on the farm and knew that my staff would take care of things in London. The following day, my entire staff, four hundred guests, including hundreds of brightly dressed Punjabi-Indians, and numerous hippy friends, assembled on the land together to celebrate our marriage. It was during this time that Sundeep and I were also able to announce the result of the award, much to the excitement of our friends, family and colleagues.

The party lasted for three days with people camping out on the land. My father-in-law, a master Indian classical musician, and his fellow artists played live on stage. Friends of ours, who are well known DJs, then played late into the night and through to the early hours in the remote and beautiful valley in East Sussex, where we live. We all celebrated the marriage and felt great about the award.

The party was wonderful and unforgettable. None of us however could have predicted the huge media attention and national acclaim which would follow the success of the award over the coming months.

Immediately after the award, the school received some significant media coverage. The *TES* published a very positive story about the school which was followed by a prominent article in *The Times*. People across the country were beginning to hear about the school with a herd of water buffalo and the headteacher who rides around the school grounds on a quad bike.

The response to these stories on social media was extensive. It reflected a powerful appetite on behalf of the British public and around the world for teachers and children to be liberated from what they perceived to be as a limiting health and safety culture within schools.

I began to receive emails and letters from people within the profession and from members of the general public asking to visit the school and congratulating us on what we had achieved. They perceived the work of the school as revolutionary and felt that we were breaking the mould.

Further national press coverage followed in the Telegraph, BBC Radio and BBC Television News, which again sparked enthusiasm across the country for what we were doing. People were still saying however that we were bucking against a trend which had been created by the Government, the HSE and Ofsted and that somehow we were being rebellious. Amongst all the very positive coverage for the school, it was still incorrect about where the cotton wool culture had really originated from.

I make sure that my health and safety knowledge is up-to-date because I am the health and safety co-ordinator for my school; I am ultimately responsible for the whole site and for the safety of everyone who enters it. It was whilst attending my latest health and safety course, where I learnt about the legal implications of death and injury at work, that my school office rang to say that the Health and Safety Executive were on the phone.

The course facilitator had just been telling the delegates about the length of time leaders in business and schools would be spending in prison following breaches of health and safety law. He had also pointed out that I was missing some essential signage to warn people about the water buffalo on the marsh, making me feel slightly nervous to say the least. So I was concerned that the HSE might be contacting me with a complaint.

However, to my delight and relief, I was not in some sort of trouble for a serious breach of health and safety. The phone call revealed that the National Chair of the HSE, Dame Judith Hackitt, wanted to join forces with me to tell the British public the truth about health and safety in schools with the help of the national press.

Dame Judith had read about the school in *The Times* and saw this as an opportunity to dispel a few health and safety myths with our support. I loved the idea of collaborating with the HSE and immediately said yes.

The HSE set up two interviews to keep the story exclusive, one with *The Times* and another with BBC Television News.

We decided to show the nation in a hands-on way that taking risks and exposing children to danger in a responsible manner is a good thing to do and that it is completely supported by the HSE. I designed a complete day of activities with the children for Dame Judith to engage in and for the TV crew to film at the same time.

Dame Judith's message

Setting up a day of activities was relatively easy to do because we had been working with two TV crews the week before. One was BBC's *Countryfile* and the other was Henry Ward and his crew from Freelands Foundation. They were both documenting the experiential work we do at the school and wanting to share it with a wider audience. Henry's documentary "School by the Marsh" has been seen in 95 countries since it was made and was premiered at Tate Modern in London. BBC's *Countryfile* was viewed by over nine million viewers, so the message was beginning to roll out in a very big way.

The experiential day out on the marsh was designed to explore aspects of our Bronze Age project and included children smelting tin and copper to make bronze, flint knapping, foraging for food, dying and spinning wool from our sheep, lighting fires for cooking, using knives to make spears, making bows, arrows and pots from clay from the marsh and firing them next to the open fire.

Dame Judith came to the school and took part in every one of these activities alongside the children whilst the BBC filmed it all. Dame Judith, the BBC and the children then jumped in the back of the school trailer and were pulled by Alex in the tractor to go and feed the water buffalo.

We stopped off en route to visit our bee sanctuary to see how the children actively take part in beekeeping. The tractor also visited the British Association of Shooting and Conservation (BASC), who were teaching our children to shoot clay pigeons on the marsh using guns. Children as young as ten were firing clays out of the sky with shotguns.

As you can see from the list of risky activities, there was nothing we were hiding from the HSE or from the media and deliberately organised as many activities as we could to show the nation the potential for exciting teaching and learning.

Dame Judith and I were interviewed about the reason we were collaborating during which Dame Judith, as the representative of the HSE, was asked whether certain activities were banned. The list of "banned" activities in schools were among the most common media myths which had been perpetuated over the years and included children playing conkers and snowball fights. Dame Judith made it clear that these activities have never been banned by the HSE and were the product of misrepresentation in the national press. She was filmed with the children shooting shotguns, making fires and feeding the water buffalo. She endorsed every activity we engaged in. Most notably, she said that other schools should be embracing risk and danger in a calculated and responsible manner and that the HSE and misinformation were being used as an excuse not to do so.

The BBC News item was followed by a very good piece on BBC's *Countryfile* with John Craven and the short film commissioned by Elisabeth Murdoch's charity Freelands Foundation. Once again, the response was magnificent. Teachers and parents were extremely positive from across the globe and showed how strongly they wanted their children to have real, exciting experiences while managing risk and danger. We were being endorsed everywhere and by some highly respected educationalists, including the legendary Sir Ken Robinson who had seen the Freelands film in Los Angeles and praised the school on Twitter.

Dame Judith explained to the press that coping with risk and danger is crucial to a child's education and should become a key part of the school curriculum. She said that children were suffering under an "excessively risk-averse" culture in schools and that this was not preparing them adequately for later life. Dame Judith noted that children should be encouraged to climb trees and to play games where there might be a risk of injury.

Later at a speech she made at the Royal Academy of Engineering, she was highly critical of the risk-averse culture in schools, which she said was "nonsensical". She called for an end to this culture of fear that she described as "bureaucratic".

Later in the same speech, Dame Judith said that "overprotective parents and risk-averse teachers who do not enable children to learn to handle risk will lead to young adults who are poorly equipped to deal with the realities of the world around them, unable to discern real risk from trivia, not knowing who they can trust or believe". Making reference to later life and the workplace, Dame Judith added that children would become "a liability in any workplace if they do not have those basic skills to exercise judgment and take responsibility for themselves."

Her point was that the overbearing health and safety culture in schools was shielding children from even the most minor risks and that this was preventing them from learning about the real world.

What Dame Judith said on behalf of the HSE should be enough for any teacher, school leader, governing body or parent to realise that no one is stopping children from engaging in the real world and embracing risk and danger. The only people who are preventing children from having these experiences are the people making the decisions about these activities in schools. These decisions are the result of people's fears and believing everything that is written in a newspaper. Furthermore, the most senior organisation responsible for health and safety in the country actively wants us to embrace risk and danger with our children in an intelligent and conscientious manner.

Ideas for Teachers

Strangely, even after all of the positive press, some people still think that what we are doing at West Rise is somehow rebellious and that we are going against the grain regarding health and safety. This is simply untrue and the most important thing school leaders, teachers and parents can do is to understand and accept that there are no official obstacles to children engaging in risky or dangerous activities. Once everyone does this, children will be given the educational opportunities that they deserve. As Dame Judith said very clearly, it is individual schools who are choosing not to expose their children to risk and danger and not the HSE who are stopping them.

Forest School training, as mentioned before, is a good method if you are still feeling a bit reticent. You will receive a nationally recognised qualification and plenty of guidance on completion of the course. Alternatively, if money is an obstacle for teachers to be trained in Forest School skills, you can begin with smaller projects and then grow from there. Remember that it is as much a state of mind and attitude towards risk and danger as it is about taking part in the risky activities themselves. The trust and freedom I described in the previous chapter needs to be afforded to ourselves as much as we are offering it to our children.

Ofsted

The other group of people to be blamed for us not being able to give our children the experiences we believe they deserve is the UK inspectorate, Ofsted.

Having a creative approach to teaching and learning, being innovative and unique and trying out new things is actually something which Ofsted appreciate, provided that there is a measurable and positive impact on children. No matter how creative or unique the curriculum, if the impact on learning and the development of the child is minimal, then something is wrong.

Creativity is also completely compatible with the new curriculum and with every Government education initiative that I am aware of. As long as the school can explain why they do things in a particular way and can demonstrate how this benefits children and raises standards, schools can be as unusual and creative as they wish.

Ofsted no longer expect teachers to teach in a prescriptive way or make judgments about a particular style or approach. All they want to see is that whatever you are doing raises standards. Who can really argue with that?

In November 2013, West Rise Junior School had its fourth successful Ofsted inspection in nine years. It was carried out under the latest rigorous inspection criteria and within an education climate which many teachers and the media were describing as restrictive and Victorian. These were the Gove days when the rhetoric around education was as negative as it is today.

As you have already seen, West Rise Junior School is unconventional to say the least. Apart from in Asia, where you might find a herd of water buffalo roaming around the school grounds, West Rise is unique in homing these particular beasts. We manage and finance an enormous farm and environmental area while teaching the children to shoot guns. Again, apart from in the independent sector, we are the only school to do this in the country.

Every pupil is taught to light fires outside, to use knives and some even know how to cook a pigeon, which they have plucked and gutted themselves, over an open fire. We have a creative arts studio that fosters a creative autonomy where children can direct their own learning; one that is run by a committee of children rather than the conventional model of top-down adult authority. In addition to water buffalo and bees, we have sheep, pigs, chickens, ducks (geese at Christmas) and "conventional" cows. We have an operational darkroom for photography, radio studio and Mongolian yurt for Circle Time and philosophy for children.

As mentioned in the previous chapters, the pupils have been helping to construct historical replica buildings on our marshland. They also learn to hunt with gun dogs and ferrets and often go fly fishing on the marsh.

Ofsted, in their 2013 inspection of the school, gave us the grade of Outstanding for Behaviour and Safety. This was based in part on these exciting curriculum opportunities at the school, including the marsh, clay pigeon shooting and water buffalo. We were judged to be Good in the three other categories. The report made many references to our innovative projects and the very positive impact they have had on the children's learning and progress. The report stated that, "the school makes very good use of its unique site. The curriculum promotes all aspects of pupils' spiritual, moral, social and cultural development extremely well, providing pupils with many different, exciting experiences". Regarding the use of shotguns, they said, "pupils also benefit from a large variety of after-school clubs, including different sports and physical activities such as cheer-leading, capoeira and, occasionally, clay-pigeon shooting".

The Ofsted team were extremely thorough and conducted a number of lesson observations, work scrutiny and interviews with staff and children. The lead inspector, on the first day, spent the afternoon on the marsh, met the water buffalo and saw the children learning outside. He returned completely inspired.

In his report, he wrote that the children "also fully understand how to keep safe from potential hazards relating to the school's environment, knowing, for example, that the presence of reeds indicates deep water". This was written after the lead inspector started to walk towards a dyke concealed by tall reeds. He would have probably fallen in if a child hadn't warned him about the presence of deep water where reeds are growing. This reflects exactly what Dame Judith was saying when she was urging for schools to embrace risk and danger. There is no way that the child would have known about this particular danger unless they had been exposed to it themselves. When I asked Helen, our Forest School Leader about this, she was able to confirm that in a previous session she had taught the children about the deep water and reeds. The children had explored the area, discovered the site and nearly fallen in themselves.

Meanwhile, the additional inspector sat in a circle in our Mongolian yurt, hearing the children share their feelings, focus and meditate on their positive visualisations, returning to class feeling great. Each time the inspectors experienced an aspect of the provision, they would triangulate their investigations with interviews and work scrutiny. No stone was left unturned. The inspector's report stated, "pupils say that they enjoy school a great deal and are extremely proud of it. They are very keen to tell visitors about its special features and how much they benefit from them, and are articulate and self-confident without being in the least arrogant".

This positive experience of Ofsted, within our unconventional school, is not a one-off. In 2008, we had another full inspection which was also very positive. The inspectors were able to see how our unusual approach to teaching and learning benefitted the school and praised Room 13 in particular. They said that Room 13 contributed significantly to the spiritual dimension of the school in the form of awe and wonder about the world. A themed inspection on assessment in 2010, led by an HMI, also highlighted the success of our creative curriculum.

Impact and evidence

The key for us every time has been to show the inspectors evidence that what we do benefits the children. This is achieved through careful and accurate data analysis. We are able to show through our data that our provision, from the arts through to animals and Bronze Age activities, has a direct impact on raising standards across the curriculum. Our SATs results improve year on year and our internal data shows exactly the same thing. Of course as a junior school, there are some years where the data fluctuates or where we have to show that progress data is good using only our internal data. However, a robust system for assessment and plenty of evidence are hard to argue with. This information is shared and understood by the teaching staff, governors and all other relevant stakeholders. Crucially, it is the children themselves who are able to articulate and demonstrate the impact our activities have on their learning. This year the school achieved the highest SATs results in reading, writing and mathematics in the whole of Eastbourne and reached the top 5% in the country.

I have also made it as easy as possible for the inspectors to see what they need to see. I always prepare a brief document summarising the provision and its benefits, clearly presented and copied for each inspector on their arrival. This highlights our strengths and weaknesses in reading, writing and mathematics. It also shows the areas for development within teaching, in light of work scrutiny and lesson observations carried out by myself and other senior leaders. The SEF (School Evaluation Form) is longer than most, but is published on the school website, along with the SDP (School Development Plan), for Ofsted to see in advance of an inspection. This saves them time and demonstrates that the school is open and honest about its strengths and areas to work on. I have also ensured that my senior leaders and governors have read, understood and can articulate this information. Staff and governors have also been instrumental in monitoring and evaluating the school and generating reports for the SEF and SDP. My deputy, Emma Timperley, and school advisor, Bryan Meyer, have both been instrumental in the organisation and delivery of this approach. It is hard work on a day to day basis and I need to keep my staff feeling positive and seeing the relevance of playing the game in this way, but when we receive a successful Ofsted, everyone reaps the benefits.

The political landscape has changed several times since 2013, but still there are messages from the authorities which can be capitalised on. Members of the Government, such as the previous Home Secretary and Education Minister, have been talking about grit and resilience and the importance of building these traits within young people. Here we have a clear endorsement to engage in activities such as Forest School, which build character and strengthen children on many levels. I do not believe that there are any obstacles to schools wishing to do risky or dangerous activities, provided they are carried out responsibly and openly, whilst engaging with organisations such as the HSE.

Ideas for Teachers

My message to other school leaders wishing to be innovative, take risks and to do dangerous activities, is to do it! If you believe that a creative approach to teaching and learning helps children to access the curriculum and make more progress, then there is no reason not to embrace this approach. It is essential however to back this up with data and careful monitoring. If you can show Ofsted accurate evidence then inspectors will be delighted to see new things and the positive impact they have on a child's learning.

I started teaching in primary schools back in 1995 and have sustained a career within the profession for over 20 years. Every year, regardless of which Government is in power or who the Education Secretary is, I have heard complaints and excuses from within the profession about why they are not able to do what they want to do. I personally believe that if you follow your heart and do what you love, whilst also being strategic with Ofsted and the requirements of the government, then teachers are able to do whatever they like provided it has a measurable and positive educational impact on the children.

There are many occasions when you have to do things differently in education. If you do the same thing in the same old way, time and again, you will always get the same outcome. Change the way that you do things and you will get a different outcome. Last year, I asked for volunteers from my staff to become tutors in mathematics for the first time. This was because the standard and expectation within mathematics had been significantly raised by the government. Additionally, the children were to be tested in the SATs before the skills and knowledge could be fully embedded. As a result of my request, I had 18 volunteers from my staff, including myself, who tutored children in mathematics before and after school for three months. The result was that the school achieved the highest percentage of children reaching the national standard and beyond in the local area. Similarly, a robust and focused approach to teaching grammar, resulted in an equally positive outcome.

So, be prepared to do things differently and to experiment. Most of all, be positive and work hard, but try not to demonise Ofsted. If you are making a positive and measurable impact, regardless of how unconventional you may be, Ofsted will support you.

Chapter 4

Cultivating Grit and Resilience

Moving children out of their comfort zones

More than fears of what the HSE will do or what Ofsted might say, the biggest barrier to children having magnificent experiences is the low expectation teachers and parents have of the children in their care.

I recently drove my mud splattered Land Rover to the far side of the marsh where we teach our children shooting, fishing and beekeeping. It was raining hard and the ground was heavily waterlogged. A group of 16 children aged nine were lighting fires, gathering wood and erecting shelters with sticks and tarps. I joined them by the fire to have a chat and for them to make me a hot cup of coffee. Despite being wet and cold, all of the children, most of whom were girls, were smiling, happy and getting on with the job at hand. This may come as a surprise, given the harsh weather conditions, but we have come to expect this positive attitude from our children at West Rise. This is because, as a school, we have taught the children to be resilient and to venture out of their comfort zones.

The concept of people having a "comfort zone" was first conceived by psychologists Robert M. Yerkes and John Dodson more than a 100 years ago. After many experiments, they concluded that "a state of relative comfort created a steady level of performance". This state of relative comfort is the "comfort zone".

However, if a person wants to increase their performance levels and to develop personally they need to step into a state of relative anxiety where their stress levels are slightly higher than normal. The psychologists labelled this state, "optimal anxiety," which lies just beyond our comfort zone.

Since becoming the headteacher of West Rise Junior School, as well as the Special Educational Needs Co-ordinator in 2004, I have observed a steady increase in discussions amongst professionals and parents about children's perceived limitations, often sighting that they are anxious or lacking in self-esteem. I have also seen an increasing number of parents "diagnosing" their children with various disorders using internet questionnaires, simply because their children do not like change or they struggle in certain situations. The discussions have largely depended on what has been shown recently on television and therefore sparking people's fears and influencing their views. This is not to say that some children do not suffer from anxiety or struggle with change, but it is definitely the case that some parents and professionals project their own limiting beliefs and traits on to the young people in their care.

I recognise that this may be controversial for some people to read, however I have had conversations with teachers and educational psychologists from across the country who have felt the same way but are too scared to talk about it. I am convinced that in the future adults will be seeking compensation from local authorities and external agencies for inaccurately labelling them with debilitating traits when they were children, which have then negatively affected their lives.

I believe that there is currently a trend for some parents and education professionals to interpret the effects of life's challenges on children and label them with some sort of problem. This is in contrast to a culture where adults expect children to overcome their fears, build resilience and exceed expectations. An attitude to life fostered by my parents' generation and of those before them. My parents, both of whom are in their 80s, grew up in the war years. My dad, the son of working class Irish immigrants and living in Manchester, was never evacuated from the city and remembers the Germans dropping bombs on his street in Droylsden. My mother was from a more affluent background and was evacuated to Canada, although this didn't stop the Germans from trying to torpedo the ship she was on. Similarly, my great grandfather on my father's side lied about his age during the outbreak of the First World War and found himself fighting in the trenches at the Battle of the Somme at the age of 15. I often wonder how the younger generations would fair in the face of such adversity. I am not saying that children should be made to struggle, but I do feel that we should have higher expectations of them and of ourselves.

There is no doubt whatsoever that some children do suffer from anxiety and depression and many children are accurately diagnosed with Autistic Spectrum Disorder, among other significant disorders. These children are then given the extra support that they need at home and at school. There are also other times when it is the parents themselves who don't like change or who are anxious or depressed. Fuelled by misinformation on the internet and television, they then project these dynamics and fears onto their children. This dilutes the focus away from the children who genuinely need their support.

Throughout my years of teaching, I have seen many children who have been labelled with some kind of mental health issue or limiting trait, from anxiety through to lack of self-confidence, fear of change or depression. I have then observed the same children working outside in nature, in which they are not being labelled and where they are expected to rise to a particular challenge. More often than not, these children have demonstrated skills and attributes which were previously unobserved and shown confidence and courage, exceeding their own and others' limiting beliefs.

I believe that getting children outside in all weathers, giving them new and expansive experiences, having high expectations of them and demanding resilience is what many children want and need. Having an aspirational "They can do it!" approach rather than a weak "they are unable to do this" attitude, helps push children out of their comfort zones and towards fulfilling their potential.

The culture of expecting every child to have some sort of psychological problem has got to end, especially if it appears that it has more to do with their parents' or teachers' fears and obstacles. What is even more worrying is when the concerns raised are the result of the media playing on people's anxieties.

For those children who are accurately diagnosed with autistic spectrum disorder, ADHD or are depressed, West Rise has integrated and worked with these children too. I can recall several examples of children who I have been told will "not be able to cope" with working outside in the rain because they are autistic or cannot be trusted with a knife or a gun. These children in particular exceed everyone's expectations every time. With appropriate support and a watchful eye, but even more importantly with trust in the young person and with high expectations, these children are able to enjoy learning which has an element of risk and danger just as much as their peers.

It is interesting, as I wrote earlier, that people generally assume that I am the headteacher of a nice little private school for middle class kids when I tell them about the activities I do with the children at my school. The school is populated primarily with children from working class backgrounds and every year group has children within it who are accurately diagnosed with ASD. Yet we engage in activities with an element of significant risk and danger with every child in the school. As a result, the children achieve, thrive and succeed.

After three hours of hard work in the rain and while completely wet and muddy, my Year Four children were still smiling after my visit with them. The long walk through the marshes back to school still lay ahead of them, but those children all had an aura of achievement and power about them. They had adopted attributes which, if encouraged, will serve them well throughout their lives in a world full of change and uncertainty. They had stepped out of their comfort zones and into that place where they can grow and achieve. A place where they can ultimately live their dreams and go beyond the constraints of others' beliefs about them. Two of the children in the group were officially diagnosed as being on the autistic spectrum, although the parent helpers who did not know them could never have known that.

It is important that we have high expectations of the children in our care and have a positive and aspirational outlook with regards to what they can do. I have had children with ADHD handle guns proficiently. I have had children who are low-attaining writers suddenly write magnificently after being immersed in nature. I have had girls who have run away from bees in the playground have thousands of them crawling all over them after lifting the lid off a hive, whilst wearing protective clothing. People have limitless potential and children deserve to be seen as capable of reaching their potential and then exceeding it.

Carefully managed exposure to risk and danger will enable children to have new experiences and to move beyond their comfort zones. Like a flower opening up, once they return to normal life, they will have expanded that little bit more. Each time they step outside of the comfort zone they expand again, building on their confidence and enthusiasm for life. It isn't always easy, but that is the whole point.

Ideas for Teachers

There will always be a child in every class who the teacher feels will not be able to handle risk or be able to be trusted in a dangerous environment or situation. Assuming that the teacher has positive behaviour management skills, is well organised and takes full responsibility, there is no barrier to that child engaging in "dangerous" activities. The best way is to simply do it. Trust and high expectations must come first and must not be waited for. A child will know if they are trusted or not. The power of that trust, or lack of it, goes a very long way indeed and will often dictate the outcome.

Choose your groups carefully and have a balance of children who are known to be capable and responsible, with one or two who you have to keep a closer eye on. Usually, the "naughty ones" are thrown in to a group of their own and as everyone predicted they mess around and are told that they can never be trusted again. This is an example of poor management and a self-fulfilling prophecy. It is important to be one of those parents or teachers who believes in the child and is willing to give them a chance with the best possible conditions for success.

If it is a child on the autistic spectrum, pair them with an adult who enjoys being outside and wants to be there themselves. Prepare the child by telling them what they will be doing and show them photographs and videos of what they will do. Most of all, be really positive about the activities and tell them how brilliantly they are doing and have the highest possible expectations for success.

However, before you can expect children to move out of their comfort zones you need to be willing to move out of your own one first.

Moving adults out of their comfort zones.

School leaders need to cultivate the same confidence, trust and resilience that we expect of the young people in our care. If we are expecting children to step up to the mark and to become more resilient, then we need to show them these qualities within ourselves and to lead by example. Life is sometimes very challenging, but therein lies the magic and the point of embracing risk and danger. In order for us as adults to move out of our own comfort zones we need to accept that things will not always work out. This is where the real learning is for those of us within the profession and the driving force for our own self-development and expansion.

I am focusing specifically on school leaders because teachers and parents are often enthusiastic about risk-taking, but headteachers, senior leaders and governors are sometimes more reticent due to their accountability should something go wrong.

From buying a herd of water buffalo, to teaching the children clay pigeon shooting, I have had lots of ideas as a headteacher which have included an element of risk and danger.

I firmly believe that personal qualities such as optimism, courage and self-belief are hugely beneficial to risk takers and to the success of their innovations. Taking full responsibility for the successes and inevitable challenges created by taking risks is even more important. Without these personal traits, it is unlikely that a school leader will ever take any real risks.

West Rise Junior owns a herd of water buffalo on its marshland, which pupils help look after.

Year 5 children thatching the roof of the roundhouse.

Year 6 children building the raised wooden causeway.

Children lighting a fire at Forest School.

An aerial view of the roundhouse.

West Rise children learning clay pigeon shooting. Photo by Russell Sach.

Children at Forest School using home-made bows and arrows.

Children with the ducks and sheep on the main school site.

Trekking across the marsh.

Year 5 children paddle boarding on the school lake.

Learning archery.

Activities for children include beekeeping.

Children from the school entering the roundhouse which they helped to build.

By definition, a risk is a situation involving exposure to danger. As teachers, we have become skilled at writing risk assessments as part of managing the health and safety of our schools. We think carefully about what might cause harm to our pupils and staff, then we assess whether we are taking reasonable precautionary steps.

If they are created and followed properly, risk assessments, insurances, notifying relevant authorities and good communication with our stakeholders will be enough to limit the potential harm caused as a result of taking calculated risks. This will be discussed further later on in the book.

The general public and the media sway between praise and criticism for risk takers and their innovations.

In 2012, the British media praised the Health and Safety Executive and the Play Safety Forum for criticising the "cotton wool culture" of Britain, which had steadily evolved in the country for years. They reported that too many health and safety regulations imposed by government were preventing children from playing freely and exploring the world. We have seen this repeated again by Dame Judith Hackitt in 2016, fully supported by the general public and the British media.

In contrast to this, the public and the media will also articulate their concerns and can be highly critical of risk takers and their innovations at times, saying that we are being irresponsible. I have been on the receiving end of both praise and criticism, both in the end have served me well.

The reality is that you cannot always predict how things will turn out, particularly with regards to the perceptions of others. In light of this, I would like to advocate the idea of embracing failure and mistakes and will share a few of my own with you. It is the fear of making mistakes which sometimes prevents schools from embracing risk and danger. The American artist, writer and philosopher Elbert Hubbard famously said, "The greatest mistake you can make in life is continuously fearing you will make one".

For several years I have taught my pupils to fire shotguns and to learn how to retrieve ducks and pheasants with gun dogs. These experiences definitely have their educational merits in my view and are exceptional experiences for the children. Very well supported by the British Association of Shooting and Conservation (BASC), children have been taught about gun safety and gun law as well as the serious consequences of misuse of a firearm.

The philosophy behind this is multi-faceted but all of it is about education. Even if you are a vegetarian you will be directly benefitting from management of the countryside with shotguns and air rifles. There are approximately 65 million pigeons in the British countryside, as well as several million rabbits. As lovely as they are, they are not all native to our countryside and we no longer have as many predators as we would have had even a few 100 years ago. Humans therefore have become the top predator within the food chain. If left to eat all of the crops and seeds, we would be left with no food for humans or for the animals in our care. The rabbits and pigeons shot by the farming and shooting fraternity go back into the food chain, so nothing is wasted.

It is also worth noting that clay pigeon shooting and target practice are both Olympic sports for which Britain has gained medals, much to the delight of the national press and the public at large. Skills such as eye and hand co-ordination, focus, high expectation and commitment to the sport are all benefits of the pursuit. As with other great sports, people often begin by learning the sport when they are children.

At West Rise we teach these skills to our children in a hands-on way on the marsh with children learning to shoot guns, whilst learning about the environmental benefits. However, the critical press coverage which followed our first year of this event was both inevitable and challenging. Despite the *Times Educational Supplement* publishing a balanced and educationally sound article about the reasons why we teach our children countryside sports, other elements of the national press were highly critical.

Nonetheless, we persevered and weathered the media storm to the point where four years on BBC's *Countryfile*, hosted by John Craven, celebrated our annual countryside management event. BBC TV News and other networks similarly reported in a balanced and positive manner about what we are doing. Even the previously critical publications grew to admire what we had achieved and eventually reported our achievements in a positive light. This journey required me to step out of my comfort zone and exhibit huge resilience and grit in the face of adversity.

Resilience and the kind of steadfastness which my parents exhibited during the war years kicked in for me the week after we bought our herd of water buffalo. As mentioned earlier, I was very excited when we purchased the water buffalo and they have gone on to be the subject matter of numerous poems and artwork generated by the children. They have also helped the children to learn about animal husbandry and habitats. I was less enthusiastic however when the entire herd ran away and ended up on Eastbourne seafront, appearing on BBC Television News eating one of the neighbours' prize privet bushes! Again, by staying positive and strong in the face of adversity, the event had a happy ending. It ended up being laughed off by the press and the local community, even by the local police who had discovered the water buffalo walking along the seafront at five o-clock in the morning.

Again, I believe that cultivating a sense of optimism, courage and self-belief is essential to anyone wishing to take risks. Taking full responsibility for your successes and your failures is also very important and empowering.

You are likely to experience a whole range of responses from others to your risky ideas. This is part and parcel of taking risks. Some things will go well, whilst other aspects might not go quite to plan. I have had many of these experiences.

Another example of this was when I introduced approximately one million honey bees to my school a few years ago. Clearly an excellent idea, it has enabled my children to become natural beekeepers, helped the environment and expanded our school farm. We work alongside "bee shamans" who, they say, enter the hives in various states of trance and communicate with these magical animals on the astral plain. When the bees first arrived in several large boxes, I had not expected one of them to open up too quickly, releasing thousands of angry bees which then proceeded to chase my staff, my wife and myself around the school grounds. I was stung several times on my head, which the shamans told me was a shamanic gift and a good vibe. My wife who was stung at the same time suggested that the learning gift we might like to consider could include the idea of us wearing protective clothing before opening up a box of angry bees in the future. An idea we have since embraced wholeheartedly.

I could mention numerous other risky endeavours we have undertaken, from sending the school pig to slaughter to the school paddle boarding project. We regularly teach the children to light fires, hatch ducks' eggs in the classroom, take part in archery, use knives and make spear heads from molten metal. The list goes on.

All of our projects have had their challenges but without a doubt the benefits have always outweighed the risks and each project has had a powerful, positive and lasting educational impact on the pupils at my school.

Children deserve to have real and exciting experiences during their education, so that they can learn deeply and develop a love of life. It is the responsibility of the adults around them to create these opportunities and to do this we will inevitably be required to take risks ourselves, even if they don't always go to plan.

I would like to conclude with a real legend and example of true grit. Someone who makes me step up to the mark every time I think about what he does. Professor Sital Singh Sitara is an 80-year-old Punjabi-Indian gentleman living in East London. He goes to work every day, seven days a week, travelling on the London Underground and Overground networks to various Sikh temples and schools around London and beyond. There he teaches adults and children to play musical instruments. He is a master sitar player, Indian classical violin player, harmonium and tabla player and singer, which he teaches to his students. He has taught three generations of British Asians, totalling over 18,000 people. Additionally, Mr Sitara is a priest within his faith and performs marriages and funerals, as well as religious celebrations on a weekly basis. He has committed the Sikh holy book to memory in order for him to do this. Most astonishingly is the fact that Mr Sitara has been completely blind in both eyes since the age of three and yet he travels to his numerous work places without the help of a guide dog or human assistance, rain or shine. I know his story very well indeed because Mr Sitara is my father-in-law and I have seen him go off to work on the Tube, carrying his musical instruments and returning home for years.

So the resilience, grit and inner strength I have advocated is enshrined to epic proportions in this man. When I think about what he achieves on a daily basis, it makes me feel like I have no excuse for failure or lack of courage.

We can probably all find someone within our lives or an individual we may have read about or seen on television, someone who inspires us to move beyond what we thought we were previously capable of. Whoever our inspiration may be, it is important for us to be examples of the change we wish to see in the world.

Like the children in our care, adults also need to move out of their comfort zones at times in order to embrace risk and danger. Rather than fearing failure in doing so, we need to embrace it and see mistakes as a necessary part of our development.

Ideas for Teachers

Firstly, find a character in real life or in fiction who inspires you to be better and stronger than you thought you could be. Examine the traits of this character and adopt them as you would do if you were to role play the character when embarking on brave new projects.

Ensure that the language you are using around children and your peers is positive and aspirational. Similarly, ensure that the language you use to describe yourself and in your inner thoughts is also positive and aspirational.

Finally, mind map or list the projects you would love to be able to do, but which you have previously felt fearful about embracing. Begin one of them today. Once you have begun, you will have moved out of your comfort zone and you will expand. Even if it does not go completely to plan, you will have achieved part of your dream and you can do it even better next time.

Building grit and resilience with natural chemicals

As previously mentioned, the government and education professionals have been talking a lot about character building recently, as well as resilience and grit within young people. There is also a new drive to combat depression and create happier children. It is absolutely right to promote these qualities within young people. As I have already discussed, it makes sense for these same qualities to be demonstrated by adults within the profession if young people are to follow suit.

I would like to offer another perspective on this related to how we feel physically, emotionally and mentally. Resilience, perseverance and grit do not just appear in a person, they have to be cultivated and there is a chemical process within the body which underpins this. These chemicals are enhanced as a result of creating certain conditions and habits, which if understood and harnessed, will build character within a person and lead to a happier life.

I was recently observing an art lesson in Year 6, in which the children were drawing skulls, plants and feathers collected from the marsh. The feeling of well-being and positivity generated by the teacher and her children was physically tangible. Even the SATs revision in the neighbouring class was made to be exciting and engaging, due to the expertise and heart-centred approach of the teacher. I felt like I was bathing in a golden light and good vibes.

The question is, why would SATs revision make me feel this great? A few hours earlier, I was at home with my wife. We live apart during the week, with my wife teaching at the University of Law in London and me running my school on the South Coast. As a result, we have the most fabulous and romantic weekends together so that Mondays, after a weekend of quality time with my wife and family, always feel great! The great feeling can be attributed to a chemical called oxytocin.

Oxytocin, sometimes called the "love hormone", is usually triggered in the brain by physical contact with a loved one and has a positive impact on all other relationships, including those at work. It can also be released through massage, yoga and any harmonious contact with another person. I feel that my very beautiful and inspiring wife is responsible for a large amount of the love hormone within my system and the happy feeling then inspires me when I am at work. This contributes hugely to the sense of optimism I feel when embarking on risky or dangerous projects, even in the face of adversity.

It's not that we are without our challenges at the school. The increased demands of the National Curriculum, SATs and Ofsted are all as serious for us as for any other school. This is where the next chemical kicks in, dopamine.

Dopamine is often called the "motivation molecule". It helps us achieve our goals and to focus. It is essential for cultivating the traits of resilience and grit and also creates feelings of euphoria. I believe that high dopamine levels within my own body are part of the reason I remain positive about the challenges I face as a headteacher. Anyone can increase their dopamine levels by eating foods such as avocados, bananas, meat and poultry, almonds and pumpkin seeds. Any kind of exercise from walking or swimming can also increase your dopamine levels. I ensure that I go to the gym every day. I also swim and go running. This keeps my mind focused and, again, creates the right mindset when embarking on risky and dangerous projects.

The next helpful chemical on the road to a happier life is serotonin. This regulates our mood and is boosted by a healthy diet and exercise. I love spending time outside with my pupils on our school farm and feel this boosts my serotonin levels and general happy mood. Education professionals don't always do regular exercise and we can also easily slip into poor eating habits, drinking too much coffee, not enough water and too many poor quality foods such as biscuits and cakes. Turning this around is scientifically proven to create a more positive attitude, with feelings of happiness and optimism within the people willing to embrace the change. It is also something we should be leading by example for the children within our schools. Childhood obesity and depression are on the rise. Going outside and being an example of excellent health are good for the children in our care.

The last chemical group to mention are endorphins, which naturally occurs within the body. They create a positive feeling in the body and mask pain, it is essential to character building in relation to endurance and courage. Like serotonin, eating well and exercising increases endorphin levels. They are also released when engaging in any activity which a person finds pleasurable. Positive thoughts and affirmations, massage, being in nature and meditation can all increase endorphin levels. Conscious deep breathing has also been proven to top up endorphins within the body, leading to happy feelings and a general feeling of well-being. Of course going to the gym is not always the first thing on your mind when you finish work or at the start of the day and it can feel physically painful at times. However, this is where as professionals we have to show our own resilience and grit. There is a lot to be gleaned from the saying "no pain, no gain". The chemical and emotional benefits, as well as the benefits to overall health, are undeniable.

In a way, the attributes of resilience, perseverance and happiness are all the products of other things, such as lifestyle and attitude. I firmly endorse the promotion by government of these qualities within young people and there are plenty of examples of heroic true grit within the older generation. Between 2013 and 2016, Ernie Andrus ran across America from the West to the East Coast. He was raising money for a World War Two naval landing ship to be taken across the sea to Normandy for a D-Day celebration in 2019. The incredible thing about Ernie, as well as running that great distance, is that he is 93 years of age. He is also the last surviving crew member of the ship which he plans to take to Normandy. People who are less than a quarter of this man's age would find this goal massively challenging yet Ernie, who is almost a century old, managed to achieve this incredible feat through sheer perseverance.

By understanding the chemical mechanics of happiness and wellbeing whilst applying them to ourselves and to the children in our care, we will then be able to increase feelings of wellbeing, strengthen our character and step out of our comfort zones more effectively.

Ideas for Teachers

Embarking on risky and dangerous activities requires you to be fully focused and prepared. You may need to be physically fit if you are out on the land with the children in all weathers and, most importantly, you need to have a positive attitude and outlook.

Everything I have described in this chapter is part of the jigsaw which enables individuals and organisations to have the energy and vision to embrace risk and danger. Good mental, physical and emotional health are important characteristics for an adult to have if they work with children. I urge schools to consider a culture change with regards to its approach to fitness. Have fruit and not just biscuits in the staff room and encourage each other with regards to fitness and health.

Join a gym and make yourself go to it. Even a few lengths in a swimming pool each day, or a run around the block in the morning, will change the way your day goes and will make you feel great.

If you are in a position of responsibility and influence within the school, appoint people with a passion for physical exercise who may be able to influence the school. Two years ago I appointed Emily Kitchos, a young teacher who is also a water sports and ski instructor. Within her first year at West Rise, she accessed funding in order to buy seven stand up paddle boards for use on our school lake. Now every child within the school learns to stand up paddle board and soon they will be taught sailing. Emily has also recently bought a class set of mountain bikes and every class is being taught to ride a bike, or to enhance their existing biking skills.

Not everyone within a school will want to do this and, at the end of the day, it is up to each individual to make that decision. Regardless, it seems fair to me that if we are expecting children to step up to the mark then we should too.

Chapter 5

Video Gaming as Inspiration

Another reason teachers and parents do not always embrace activities such as those we have introduced at West Rise is because they say that children will not be interested in them as they are too involved with their computers. As a headteacher and parent of teenage boys, I have witnessed a huge cultural divide between young people who play video games and the adults in their lives. I felt some of this separation between my son and myself, until I took the time to understand his world and saw the educational opportunities and links to working outside. In terms of risk and danger, video games offer a broad spectrum of subject matter which will engage most children.

Inside the game

Three years ago I witnessed my 16-year-old son Tali crash his Reaver, a high tech hovering warplane, in the Indar Desert, a lonely and dangerous region of Auraxis, in the world of Planetside. He was an engineer working for "The Empire" and was on the battlefield alone.

His Reaver was completely destroyed but Tali was physically unscathed. He scanned the desolate terrain, within which he had found himself, when over the crest of a sand dune appeared an Armoured Personnel Vehicle (APV). Smoke was pouring from its engine and it looked battle worn and menacing. Tali assumed that the vehicle was hostile until, through his headphones, he was introduced to the colourful and jovial crew of the vehicle.

The crew of seven soldiers were playing the video game from completely different parts of the real world, whilst occupying the APV in the virtual world of Planetside 2. The highest ranking officer was talking to Tali from Germany. Two were from Holland. One introduced himself from Brazil. Two were in England and another in Denmark. The German recognised that Tali was an engineer and asked whether he would repair his APV. In return the crew would help Tali out of his predicament, by allowing him to join their crew and take him to safety. Tali agreed.

I listened to this amazing conversation whilst sitting next to my son in his bedroom in East Sussex. A meeting of cultures, enthusiasm, teamwork and respect from across the globe. A meeting which would have an extraordinary influence on my son in the future.

The benefits of gaming

I found this experience with Tali wonderfully inspiring and positive. Still, one session with an E-Safety Consultant within the school, or reports in the press about video games, leave most teachers believing that video games will cause young people to go on to rape, pillage and murder within the real world as soon as they are off the computer. There is no scientific research to back up this view and the truth is that video games can be very beneficial.

Apart from the obvious positive social interaction which I witnessed from within my son's bedroom, research shows that action video games have numerous other benefits. They involve fast motion and require the player to be aware of and react to multiple situations simultaneously. Academic studies show that playing these games improves the player's ability to multi-task in the real world, a skill which few people truly possess.

In several studies, gamers compared to non-gamers have better attention spans and are quicker to make accurate decisions than their non-gaming peers. This has a powerful impact on people's potential to learn new skills and acquire new knowledge, it has been widely researched and documented in academic journals.

Other studies have shown how gamers have compared to non-gamers within the world of work. Endoscopic surgeons who play video games outperform their non-gaming peers, even when their peers have more years' experience in surgery. Further tests demonstrate how gamers have flown and landed computer-simulated aeroplanes and drones to the same level of accuracy as real pilots.

There is also evidence to suggest that gaming significantly improves the symptoms of dyslexia. Few other activities have been reported to have such a powerful and positive impact.

Tali's younger brother, Iggy, also plays video games which simulate shooting guns. In the real world he is an excellent shot with an air rifle and frequently returns from our country garden with a pigeon, which he prepares and cooks himself for the family to eat.

Negative press

In the same way that health and safety has been demonised in the media, in education and by the public, the same is true for video gaming in my view. There are many myths and inaccuracies surrounding the subject. Having heard numerous scare stories in the press and from educationists, I decided to ask people within the games industry itself for their opinion about gamers and gaming and why there has been so much negative press.

By far the most Internationally famous and successful games critic and advocate of the hobby is John Bain (referred to online as Totalbiscuit or Cynical Brit). He is a full-time games critic who works through YouTube and Twitch TV. There is never a day when young gamers across the globe will not be listening to Totalbiscuit's views about the latest video game. I decided to ask him for his opinion on the subject of the cultural divide and this was his response:

"When most people think about gamers they think about one person alone on a console or a PC in a room. Society is very afraid of loners and imagine them stuck in a basement somewhere, plotting some awful atrocity. The reality is that this is a very outdated way of looking at gaming. Multi-player games have replaced the lone player, with tens of millions of people playing together on the same game at the same time. There is an opportunity through this to meet new people and to be exposed to new cultures. The interesting thing about this is that you often run into people from other countries. The player gets exposed to other cultures and other points of view which they may not otherwise come into contact with, especially in England where some towns are very homogenous. This improves cultural understanding at a young age and broadens horizons."

He informed me that only 14% of games are rated "M" for "Mature" by the Entertainment Software Ratings Board (ESRB). These games should only be played by people who are 17 years of age or over and this is where good parenting and guidance from teachers is required.

To gain a deeper understanding of the way games are rated I contacted Will Davis, Education Manager at the International Game Academy in Holland, who supports this view and said, "There are games with content that are not suitable for children, and these are clearly labelled with the same age ratings as films. If parents are concerned about inappropriate content, the games industry and retailers should be supported in their efforts to ensure that those age ratings are enforced throughout the supply chain. The name 'games' can suggest that all games are suitable for children, which may partially lie behind their often controversial status, but all professional games developers recognise that not all games fit all audiences."

Totalbiscuit adds further caution with regards to ensuring that young people never give out their personal information, such as names and addresses online. He also warns against excessive amounts of time playing games and advises that there must be a balance. These are things which require guidance from parents and teachers. However, parents and teachers also need to update their own knowledge about gaming and gamers and to see the educational benefits and links to working on projects in the physical world.

History repeated

It would appear to me that there has been an excessive amount of negative press about video games and this is what has informed most adults' views. Totalbiscuit believes that this is a phenomenon which has happened to other forms of media throughout history. He tells me that "there was negative press about rock and metal music and its fans in the '80s. If we go back even further, it has happened with certain books and with movies and television. Gaming is the newest form of media which has become popular and which has become stigmatised and demonised. It has become stereotyped in many ways."

He added that it is ironic to think that almost every teacher and parents plays some kind of video game on their mobile phone these days, yet probably very few of them would consider themselves to be a gamer.

Totalbiscuit ended our conversation with a powerful point about the danger of adults seeing themselves so differently from young people who play video games. "Demonising video games creates a rift between teachers and students and parents and their children. Having an outdated and negative view of video games, which the majority of children engage with, only serves to alienate young people. If you are working with children, there is no excuse not to have at least a basic working knowledge of what they are really doing, otherwise the rift will expand."

Accurate knowledge and understanding

Three years after my son met the international crew of fellow gamers on board their dilapidated vehicle within Planetside 2; Tali has developed his gaming interest with a passion. He is now studying International Game Architecture and Design at NHTV in Holland. The course teaches young artists to develop their computer graphics skills to a professional standard for the gaming industry. It is a highly creative and cutting edge field within art and design that has excellent progression into the industry. He first became interested in the field when he was in Year Six while sitting on the Room 13 committee at West Rise Junior School in the role of Communications Officer.

Tali is still in touch with some of the crew who rescued him in the Indar Desert and has met up with the Dutch crew members in Holland within the real world. They have become good friends and still play video games online to this day.

Far from being a source of anti-social behaviour, Tali's story reflects the vast amounts of scholarly and scientific research which are available about gaming. It demonstrates that gaming can be beneficial.

I believe that it is time to heal the cultural divide, which has grown between adults and young people over the use of video games, and replace it with real knowledge and understanding. It is time for us as parents and educationists to do our own research as academics and thinkers, rather than relying on popular belief and the media to inform our opinions. Exactly the same applies to our knowledge and understanding of health and safety in schools.

I believe that the possibilities regarding the links between the gaming world which children are so involved in and the real world are endless. Adults will sometimes say that children are not interested in Forest School, or roaming around the natural environment foraging for food, but only the opposite is true. Even more striking is that it is often the children who are avid gamers that will excel in activities such as shooting, archery, foraging, orienteering and problem-solving.

The problem comes when video gaming is not monitored by the adults in charge and children are not encouraged to engage with the physical world. Video games are very good at challenging the player's emotional and intellectual comfort zones, but do not challenge them physically or take them out of their physical comfort zones. It is therefore very important to give children physical challenges to push them beyond their physical limits. This can be achieved with video games as a stimulus.

Ideas for Teachers

I have noticed whilst working with children outside that they will sometimes make references to the gaming world and that this inspires further enquiry and activity within the physical world.

Throughout many of the games which I have seen, the player is constantly on the move through various landscapes, including mountainous regions, forests, caves, rivers and lakes. The landscapes often have a Tolkienesque quality about them and are steeped in ancient folklore, sometimes Nordic or Celtic. This can be easily replicated within the real natural world. For example, a local woodland can be brought to life through a Nordic storyline or problem-solving activity.

Whilst in the game the player will experience a wide range of activities. Smelting metal to make weapons is an activity which I have seen and, of course, the children do this at West Rise to make arrow and spear heads.

Some games involve food and herb gathering. Again, foraging for food within the natural environment is something we do on the marsh at West Rise and can be replicated in similar environments. Catching fish and hunting is a further activity children engage in within the virtual world. Alex has taken the children fishing with rods that the children have made from garden canes and goose feather quills from the marsh. Video games will also include hunting skills, firing arrows and shooting guns. Making bows and arrows is easy to do using willow withies and garden string. Set up a target for the children and away you go.

Some games involve fire and shelter buildings. We do this at school when working outside in the winter. You can make shelters from tarps and boxes, amongst many other materials. Your children will love to build camps and will use the materials you provide for them in surprising ways.

Cross country treasure hunts are a feature of some games. In a game called Skyrim the player has to find chests with loot in as a reward. This is easy to replicate within the physical world and can be linked to mathematical problem solving activities. Even if you just use the tarmac playground, this is an activity which is simple to deliver.

Other skills you will see within video games are alchemy, or potion-making, trading, bartering and combat skills using swords and spears. All of these are activities which can be replicated within the physical world for children to enjoy on a different level. Links to potion making can be made through science and role play fighting can be linked to history projects, such as 1066.

In some video games, I have seen huge Nordic puzzles where the player needs to turn stone circles and complete riddles to get through to dungeons etc. Again, this can be created within the real world and lends itself to large parts of the school curriculum such as mathematics. The school grounds can be brought to life through these kinds of activities.

Find out what the children you work with play on their computers and make the links within the real world. The children will love it and may surprise you with how proficient they are at learning these "new" skills.

Chapter 6

Head, Hand and Heart

I would now like to offer the reader some inspiration in the form of Bedales School in Hampshire. Like West Rise Junior School, Bedales give their children a wide range of opportunities to work outside in nature. They also have a highly creative ethos and marry the arts with working outside very well indeed. Additionally, they have developed a framework of aims and intentions, which are endorsed by the whole school community. The aims allow activities involving an element of risk and creativity to fit within a wider ideological context, thus giving them more depth and relevance. The Bedales approach also fascinates me because it is not a new vision at all but a model for education, which was conceived over a hundred years ago.

Connecting with Bedales

My first contact with Bedales was through its Deputy Head of Academic Studies, Alistair McConville. Introducing himself to me as Al, he emailed me asking whether he could visit West Rise Junior School. I receive lots of visitors to the school and I am always happy to share what we do with anyone who is interested. Visitors also bring a cross-fertilisation of ideas and new connections, which invariably lead on to new projects. My meeting with Al was one of these powerful connections.

It was a windy day in November 2015 when Al arrived at my school. I had co-ordinated the meeting with another request to visit, from a man called Henry Ward. The connection with Henry later inspired the creation of the film "School by the Marsh". This is a film about West Rise and was premiered at Tate Modern in London in 2016.

When people visit me at West Rise, I do not just sit them down in my office and talk about our projects. I like to give my visitors the real, hands-on experience of the school. This usually involves getting them on the back of the quad bike and taking them around the marsh. Al and Henry liked the sound of this, so we all boarded the machine and sped off down the road and across the fields to where my Forest School was taking place.

By now the wind had really started to pick up. Helen told us that "Hurricane Abigail" was due to hit the South Coast that morning and that Forest School might have to be cut short. Nonetheless, the two visitors and I spent a good amount of time with the pupils, sitting around the fire, which the children had made and chatting with various people. A pupil made us hot drinks and everyone talked about the activities they were engaged in. Knives were being used to whittle wood and shelters were being erected as best they could, given the worsening weather conditions.

After a while, I suggested to Al and Henry that we might like to travel across the 120 acres of marshland to try and find the water buffalo. We planned to drive around the lake and perhaps see the bee sanctuary too. As we hurtled across the marsh on the quad bike, the three of us spoke excitedly about the arts and education and the nature of our respective organisations. We were all connecting brilliantly when, over the South Downs, appeared the menacing black rain clouds of Hurricane Abigail.

Looking back, it was probably a bad idea for us to drive off into the oncoming storm, but we were feeling really excited. The three of us said later that we had all felt like little boys on an adventure at the time. An adventure which came to an abrupt end when the quad bike ground itself into several feet of thick mud. That is when the skies opened up and the torrential rain started to pour down. I hastily made a phone call to Alex, who is experienced in pulling my vehicles out of similar situations using the tractor. He eventually turned up to help us and drove us back to school. Meanwhile, the water buffalo, which we never actually managed to see, had sensibly taken refuge from the storm in their shelter on the far side of the marsh.

Despite the insane weather conditions, we all had an excellent time and still managed to plan and discuss further projects and collaborations. I had agreed to work with Henry and to give a talk at Tate Modern in February. I had also agreed to talk at a leadership conference, hosted by the *TES* at Bedales School, the following May. I felt tremendously inspired by what I had heard about Bedales and its long-standing, creative ethos, I believed that I could learn a lot from this connection.

I was particularly intrigued by the fact that the Bedales approach had been conceived over a hundred years ago, by a man called John Haden Badley and that his vision for education resonated with my own.

John Haden Badley

John Haden Badley (1865-1967) was an educator and author and the founder of Bedales School, formerly located in Haywards Heath and then moving to Hampshire. Badley is a romantic figure to any modern and idealistic educator, such as myself. His friends included Oscar Wilde and Yeats, amongst many other inspiring and creative people. He was highly political and socially aware and wished to make a difference to the world in which he lived. This is what I believe most teachers strive to do today and one of the reasons I respect Badley's work.

At the age of 24, after graduating from Cambridge, Badley became a teacher at Abbotsholme School which is a progressive school founded by Cecil Reddie in 1889. Reddie wished to create an alternative to the restrictive and more traditional public schools of the day, such as Eton. During this time, Badley formed many of his ideas about education and he soon went on to found Bedales School in 1893.

Like Reddie, Badley created Bedales as an alternative to the authoritarian approach to education which was typical in Victorian England at that time. He was a contemporary of Montessori and Steiner and was hugely influenced by their approaches to education. This helped Badley shape his vision for a school of his own.

The culture of Bedales derives from a quote by the artist and writer, John Ruskin, in which he said, "Fine art is that in which the hand, the head, and the heart of man go together." The quote is abbreviated to "head, hand and heart" referring to the holistic approach to education which is promoted throughout Bedales School.

Interestingly, like West Rise Junior School, Bedales is set within 120 acres of natural landscape. Although not a marshland, it is surrounded by trees and soft rolling hills. For the first few decades of its existence, Bedales attracted various artists and writers due to its progressive spirit which appealed to forward-thinking and creative people. In the 1960s, the school became well known for attracting creative parents, some of whom were famous artists, musicians and poets. The '60s, which were also a time of experimentation and progressive thinking, meant that Bedales offered an exciting alternative to the other forms of education which were available at that time. This seems to have been quite a formative and legendary period in the school's history.

The school's forward-thinking disposition has helped create successful artists and musicians, writers and even politicians over the years. Badley believed in his vision for young people and what they could achieve. He created a powerful example of creative education, the legacy of which continues to this day.

An innovative curriculum

When I visited Bedales School to deliver my presentation about leadership in May 2016, I was also given a tour of the school. This included a trip around the estate in Al's Land Rover and a good look at the school's facilities. Through this I gained a deeper understanding of the school's curriculum and values. I also began to appreciate the similarities between this long established approach to education and my own work at West Rise Junior School.

The conference at which I was talking was titled "Liberating Leaders". I was asked to talk about my approach to education, the history of West Rise and how I perform my role as a school leader. It was basically an abbreviated version of this book. At the end of my talk, the headteacher of Bedales, Keith Budge, said that Badley would be "doing a jig in his plus fours" if he could hear what we were doing at West Rise. I was equally inspired by the story of Badley and the innovative curriculum, which the current headteacher had continued and expanded over the years.

Bedales offers its pupils a highly creative curriculum. It also embraces risk as evidenced by over a century of ground-breaking creativity at the school. Whilst schools in England as a whole have remained fairly rigid, Bedales has managed to stay true to Badley's original progressive vision.

Like West Rise, and one of the reasons Al came to visit me, working outside in nature is integral to the Bedales experience. Activities are centred around maintaining the school's estate, including building barns, creating natural sculptures as well as building bridges and natural habitats such as ponds. Tree planting and making food from produce grown on the land is also undertaken.

When I visited to deliver my presentation, the pupils had just sent one of their pigs to slaughter and were serving sausages made from it to the audience I was about to address. Gardening and livestock management tasks are also integral to the school's curriculum. You can begin to see why this felt like a home from home to me.

Additionally, the school opened up a new art and design building in 2016 which is reminiscent to me of the art studios I used to frequent as an art student in the 1990's. The art and design building is a very impressive space where everything from blacksmithing to print making, painting and sculpture flourish. It is totally cross-curricular and links are constantly being made with the activities which the children engage in outside.

The curriculum has a very strong emphasis on the arts and students are able to learn a wide range of instruments as well as engage in visual art and design, drama and singing. Like the original Bedales founded by Badley, the modern Bedales continues to be a beacon of creativity and an excellent example of truly holistic and heart-centred education. Perhaps because this approach has been embedded over decades, the curriculum and the reasons for working in this way feel like they have deep roots. The school has enshrined this way of working in five aims for the school.

An ideological framework for risk and danger within schools

I wanted to discuss Bedales because it offers another example of how risk-taking, creativity and embracing danger can be hugely impactful on children and young people. I am highlighting this example because it is not a new thing but has been the vision of educators, such as John Haden Badley, for a very long time. Today we find that there is still a strong appetite for this way of learning from parents and teachers and yet, despite having "permission" from the HSE and the government, schools find reasons why they are not able to teach in this way.

It may inspire school leaders to adopt a more progressive approach to teaching and learning by briefly summarising the main educational aims at Bedales. Again, these aims reflect the spirit at West Rise Junior School and therefore can be successfully replicated within the mainstream.

Aim 1, To develop inquisitive thinkers with a love of learning who cherish independent thought: Bedales aims to "create an environment where questioning, divergent thinking and the freedom to learn from mistakes are all encouraged". This is clearly an excellent aim for any educational establishment to endorse. Developing children's critical and creative thinking, as well as helping them to become life-long learners. Within this aim, the school also encourages pupils to "take responsibility for their own learning, good work habits and a sense that learning can thrill and invigorate". Once these essential attributes have been adopted and mastered, individual learners can achieve anything in my view.

Aim 2, To enable students' talents to develop through doing and making: The school states that it gives students "the ability to be involved in practical spheres – hand work as opposed to head work". They also state that "we believe that within the curriculum hands-on experience should infuse our students". This is facilitated by the vast amount of opportunities on offer for pupils to work outside, looking after the animals and creating artwork and building structures on the estate. "Doing and making" is the vehicle with which individuals can find their talents and blossom. Due to the cross-curricular nature of the curriculum, doing and making also enhances other skills, including those which are purely academic. Academically the school excels.

Aim 3, To foster individuality and encourage initiative, creativity and the appreciation of the beautiful: I particularly like this aim because of the phrase "appreciation of the beautiful" If everyone adopted this attitude, then the world would be an even better and more beautiful place. This aim is facilitated by the outside activities but also through the visual arts, music and drama. Bedales say that they see the qualities of "individuality, initiative and appreciation of the beautiful as both being life-enhancing and increasingly valued in a world of work where a premium is put on intellectual capital and creativity. Individuality must flourish, but within a clear moral structure". What I like about this view and the way in which the school promotes it, is that the qualities of individuality, initiative and appreciation are cultivated through the school's outside curriculum and the creative arts. The aim also gives a moral and ideological motivation for engaging in such activities.

Aim 4, To enable students, former students, parents and staff to take pride in the community's distinctiveness and to feel valued and nourished by the community: Bedales say that "staff and students expect of each other the best kind of relationships – co-operative, authentic, trustful and tolerant ones". The element of trust, which I first discussed when talking about Room 13 at West Rise, is very clearly central to this kind of humane approach to educating children. As I have said earlier, mutual trust and a culture of freedom are essential when involving children in activities which include an element of risk and danger.

Aim 5, To foster interest beyond the school, engaging with the local community and developing a national and international awareness: This involves giving the children opportunities to work alongside others, locally, nationally and globally. I particularly like the big picture context of this aim because it sets the school within the wider context of the local and global community. This sense of belonging and community achieved, not through children sitting passively in a classroom listening to the teacher, but through hands-on experiences and creativity. This is an approach which I believe can be adopted by every school in the country. The aim is cohesive and positive and much needed in a world where individuals sometimes feel separate and polarised.

The complete set of five aims promoted throughout Bedales School, which is underpinned by Badley's original vision, give deep meaning and relevance to the activities which the children engage in. Rearing animals, performing building work, carpentry and welding metal, all involve an element of risk and danger but are not simply done for the sake of doing dangerous things. They all contribute to the sense of purpose as outlined in the aims of the school. The activities are informed by the aims and in turn, the aims are brought to life by the activities. This is an approach which school leaders and teachers might like to develop within their own practice and settings. I feel that it would give their activities, which involve risk and danger, even more gravitas and meaning.

Throughout this book, I have demonstrated how at West Rise we have educated the pupils through embracing risk and danger. "The head", or academic skills and logical problem solving attributes are developed through "the hand", or practical and physical skills and learning outside. In turn, these skills and attributes develop "the heart", or the emotional intelligence of the child. The team work, typical of Forest School, fosters empathy, as does working alongside older members of the community or through rearing animals. The head, hand and heart are all equal and all feed into one another to form the whole child. This is a powerful reason to work in this way and why we should promote it in schools.

Ideas for Teachers

The five aims promoted by Bedales are a framework within which the school community and the curriculum operates. Every school will have its own vision and set of aims and objectives. What I suggest is that headteachers and their staff examine their own school vision and aims, making links between them and the future activities which they wish to engage in.

Every school will have a behaviour policy and code of conduct which needs to be integral to any work involving risk and danger. There will also be broader ethical aspirations endorsed by the school, which again you can link in with your activities.

Remember that you are not embracing risk and danger for the sake of it but are doing it because it benefits your pupil on many levels. Make a list of the benefits and show how they are an expression of your school ethos. This will make your projects more relevant to everyone, especially to the children, parents, teachers and governors.

Chapter 7

The Impact of the Approach

The academic impact

Every year I organise an event on the marsh which spans over four complete days. I call it "Spirit of the Marsh". It is designed to support the school's study of the Bronze Age.

Last year, I invited Chris Greatorex, the archaeologist who discovered the Bronze Age site back in 2004. He talked with the children in the roundhouse about the artefacts, which he had unearthed, and answered questions about archaeology and the Bronze Age.

Every child has the opportunity to work the leather bellows to fire the earth furnace we build each year. As they pour molten metal into various moulds, their eyes light up with excitement and wonder as the metal hardens. Within minutes, the children will have made their own medallion, or arrow head out of bronze. Simultaneously, children will be learning to flint knap with expert practitioners in order to make arrow heads and scrapers for tanning hides. There will be examples of flint axe heads and bronze axe heads for the children to compare and they will learn how their ancestors made them.

Children will make natural dyes from elderberries and other plant materials after collecting them on the journey to the marsh. These are then used to dye wool from our sheep. The sheep themselves will have been bottle fed as sock lambs by the children back on the main school site the previous year. The wool is spun using spindles which the children have also made.

A large fire, which a class will have lit at the beginning of the day and further classes will have tended over each session, will be burning hot and strong. The fire is always the spiritual and physical heart of the environment within which the children are working. The children know that it gives them much needed heat when it is very cold and that it will boil the kettle for their hot drinks when making hot chocolate, coffee and tea. The children will have all learned to boil water over an open fire during Forest School sessions, which they will now be doing independently. They also prepare and cook a Bronze Age stew and cook fish which one of the parents will have caught in the sea earlier that day. Other children will be foraging for nettles and bulrush roots for cooking, whilst others will be using bows and arrows, which they have made themselves, and firing their arrows at various targets.

The inquisitive water buffalo will usually make their way across the marsh to see what the children are up to during these events, adding to the sense of awe and wonder and the feeling that we are really living in the Bronze Age.

Whatever the weather, the children will be working outside. Last year, the children were chopping wood, flint knapping and foraging in the rain and some of the smaller children were knee-deep in puddles of water, as they trekked across the land. The event was never called off due to the rain, nor because it was too cold. On one occasion three small calves, which Alex was rearing, huddled up with the children under the tarps, close to the fire.

As well as giving the children real life, hands-on experiences of what it might have been like to have lived in the Bronze Age, the experiential and elemental quality of this kind of learning has a powerful effect on children's writing. Even reluctant writer will find that their descriptive writing is ignited by the vivid experience of working outside.

Whilst out on the land, the children will learn new vocabulary when working with new tools, or whilst learning a new skill. The adults will be talking with the children constantly and asking them to describe how they feel using all of their senses. "What does it feel like?" "What can you see?" "How would you describe that sound, taste or smell?" "How does it make you feel?" There is a constant dialogue which is purposefully stimulated by the adults throughout the activities.

On return to the main school site, the children will be invited to make notes about their adventures, beginning with writing key words. They will then be asked to find metaphors for their experiences and adjectives to further enrich their writing. The children now have a strong grasp of grammar within the school which has helped give a framework for some of our weaker writers, as well as enhance the writing of our higher attaining children. They are then given the freedom to fully explore the theme of "Spirit of the Marsh" through their own thoughts and writing.

Below is an extract from a Year 6 pupil's writing which I particularly like:

"As the bracing wind rustled through my reeds, I heard the sharp, keen flint clinking together. My reedy hair swayed in the ebony sky. The pulverising footsteps of men thudded down on my dry, solid surface. A smelting bronze drifted over my verdant lands. The dancing flames whispered, overpowering the sound of the scouring flint. A galvanising shriek of a dead animal was followed by the sound of hunger in the men's voices."

Children from the estate do not usually talk like that. I am not sure anyone does. However, the magical hands-on experience of engaging in activities involving risk and danger ignited the creative spark within this 10-year-old child. He decided to talk about his experiences from the perspective of the marsh itself, which shows a maturity and sophistication that is beyond his years.

A younger child in Year 4 decided to write, not about the main activities, but about the journey to the marsh. It had started to rain and she enjoyed the classic experience of getting her wellingtons stuck in a puddle. A simple experience, but one which almost every adult can remember from childhood.

"The rain poured down at lightning speed, showing no signs of halting. When it did eventually stop, it left a rainy mist hovering in the air. Children splashed through puddles, enjoying themselves. Then the rain started again. It dampened everything, but the children's spirits. An amazingly big puddle appeared for the children to slosh through and as they did, they got their wellies stuck at the bottom. As they walked on, they felt excited about their magical day ahead."

Although not as sophisticated as the previous example, the writing is still advanced for her age and shows how her vocabulary has been enriched by the physical experience. A child getting their wellies stuck on a school trip would usually be avoided at all costs by most teachers. However, there is no hint of a chastising adult's voice within this girl's recount.

A further extract from a Year 6 girl vividly paints a picture of the weather conditions she encountered. Again, the language is powerful and descriptive and clearly the product of the real experience of being outside on a wet and windy day.

"The waterlogged marsh was tranquil. Dancing flames grew bigger in the solemn, ebony sky. The bracing wind picked up and whistled in my ear, then swirled into the time-travelling round house. The rain cascaded across my raincoat, whilst I sought refuge by the fire."

This year, our writing results were significantly above the national standard and in the top 5% of the country. Even with the demands of the new grammar curriculum, the children's writing has been brought to life by engaging in new and exciting experiences. I also believe that the riskier and more dangerous the activity, the more memorable it is and, as a result, the more a child's emotions will be engaged. If you think back to your earliest memories, they may include times when you hurt yourself falling out of a tree, or burning your finger on a match. They might be emotionally charged memories of a particular interaction with another person, or a vivid pictorial memory of a beautiful scene. Every time, the memory will have made a lasting impression because your senses were fully engaged and you were fully present in the moment. These are the conditions we seek to create when planning experiences for the children at our school. This is how embracing risk and danger can be used as a tool to support academic progress.

The children also write articles for the termly school newspaper. These articles are often inspired by their adventures on the marsh. It employs a different style of writing, which further broadens their skill and use of language.

Here is an extract from one of the reports written by a child in Year 3, aged seven.

"On Wednesday, 18th June, at midday, West Rise Marsh had an incredible delivery of a million Black Bees. They were brought carefully all the way from Wales to their brand new bee sanctuary by Clive Hedger (natural bee keeper) and his local beekeeping friends.

Amazingly, just five days before the Black Bees arrived, a wild honey bee colony decided to come into one of the hives on their own. They obviously liked the look of the beautifully painted hives.

The West Rise British Black Bee Sanctuary is a safe place for the bees to live and breed. This is important as Black Bees are endangered and almost extinct. Therefore, the ambition of the project is to provide healthy colonies of Black Bees to Sussex beekeepers.

West Rise marsh is already used for our Forest School, archery, the Bronze Age farm, the roundhouse, fishing, shooting and many other activities outside the classroom. The bee sanctuary will be part of the Bronze Age site alongside the water buffalo, cattle and roundhouse. It will give the pupils at West Rise the chance to know more about these incredible bees and how they live."

This journalistic style is quite simple but true to form, it shows the enthusiasm the child has for the provision on offer at the school. Numerous other reports are written by children from other year groups throughout the year. The newspaper has become the main newsletter to tell parents about developments at the school and is entirely written by the children. This also gives purpose to the writing, making it even more worthwhile.

The spiritual and emotional impact

I believe that giving children real and exciting experiences outside in the real world, moving them out of their comfort zones and exposing them to risk and danger also has a spiritual impact on their lives.

A good example of this has been documented by the children. As you have just read in the newspaper extract, five days before we received the bees for our bee sanctuary an extraordinary event occurred. We were holding a festival on the marsh on that day which we called "Bee Fest". Children were swimming in the lake, playing music and making bee sculptures using pine cones and other natural objects. Alex, who we trained up to be able to teach archery in-house to the children, had set up an archery range which the children were using. It was a classic summer celebration festival.

The shamanic beekeepers were on the other side of the marsh preparing the hives for our new arrivals the following day. Clive, the main bee keeper, suddenly appeared in the thick of the festival to make an announcement. He told us that during our Bee Fest, a wild swarm of honey bees had flown across the marsh and populated one of the hives.

The children in Room 13 had painted each beehive the previous week with bright colours and welcome signs for the bees. The bee shamans told us that the bees would pick up on the energy of the artwork and would feel more welcome when they arrive. The children and artists in residence entered into the spirit of this, but never guessed that a wild swarm would actually respond to the call!

Even if you are cynical about the idea of communicating with bees, I defy anyone not to be amazed and inspired by this event. For the children it was an endorsement of their hard work and love for the project. A magical experience which they will never forget. For me this is an example of true spirituality, awe and wonder.

There is also an emotional impact on children when you expose them to nature and exciting activities outside. Here are some examples of children's responses following a Forest School session. The children were all aged seven at the time.

How has Forest School affected how you feel about yourself?

- "Awesome, it's changed me in lots of ways. I loved everything."
- "It's made me feel good about going outside in nature."
- "It's changed me in a happy way."
- "It's made me happy and I've made new friends."
- "I feel that I want to start my own Forest School club. I feel happier."
- "I have enjoyed every minute of it."
- "It's made me less scared about being outside in nature."

Has Forest School affected how you feel about nature – if so how?

- "I've loved learning that stinging nettles are good."
- "I've enjoyed watching all the different animals."
- "It has inspired me about nature."
- "I like nature more now."
- "I liked nature anyway and now I love it even more."
- "I was scared of nature but it isn't scary at all."
- "I feel really happy to go out in nature, even in the rain."
- "I feel closer to it. I normally don't go out much until now. It's really cool I want to have loads to do with it."

Children start at West Rise Junior School in Year 3, which I feel is reflected in some of these responses, but they are still very genuine and demonstrate the importance of children learning outside. Feeling good about themselves and about the natural environment is a very worthy reason for providing these opportunities, regardless of any of the other benefits.

Now that schools have the full permission of the Health and Safety Executive to take their children outside to climb trees and experience nature, there is no longer any reason not to do so. Children love connecting with the natural environment, they feel positive and happy when they are outside.

Our Forest School also has very strong links with local secondary schools who send pupils to volunteer alongside our team. These children, who are at risk of exclusion from their own schools, are successfully integrated back into full time education through engaging them with working outside and empowering them to take on responsibilities. The young people eventually lead teams of younger pupils from West Rise. We are also supporting the schools we work with to start up their own Forest Schools because of the healing power that working outside has on young people. It is an investment worth making for the schools and young people alike.

Our work on the marsh has enabled children and adults to make new connections with nature and the outside environment, ensuring to visit the marsh each week for a sustained period of time. Children as young as seven will experience working in sub-zero temperatures, sweltering heat from the sun, gale force winds or will be knee-deep in mud. The enthusiasm of the group however never wanes.

There is increasing evidence to show that giving children opportunities to be outside helps with all aspects of childhood development. There are also no behavioural or special educational needs barriers to participation or to success, this approach to education is completely inclusive.

Practical skills and future employment

Schools are often criticised for not teaching children relevant practical skills in preparation for life and work. The following example from the seven-year-olds. who had also answered the previous questions, shows what practical skills they learned through our Forest School sessions.

What did you learn at Forest School?

- "How to use saws, how to be safe with things, how to use other tools and not get hurt."
- "Making things with wood."
- "That you have to work together when using a bow saw."
- "I learned how to light and tend a fire."
- "I learned how you could do anything at Forest School and for your whole life."
- "That I can cook on the fire."
- "How to use a bow saw and to be safe."

Again, these are simple responses from the seven-year-olds but they are all very powerful. These are skills and insights, which if built on during their time at West Rise, will serve the children well in the future.

In terms of what children go on to do after they have this kind of education, I have already mentioned my son Tali who has gone onto study art in Holland which was initially inspired by his time on the West Rise Room 13 committee. Other children have joined Plumpton Agricultural College just outside of Lewes, in East Sussex, with a view of entering into the farming industry. Other pupils have gone on to take up jobs in the media, dance and drama. In an area of high unemployment and inter-generational low aspiration, these are examples of the huge benefits of giving children and young people an inspiring education. Many of our activities lead to employment opportunities in the future.

Ideas for Teachers

There are lots of reasons to embrace risk and danger in schools and they are all beneficial to a child's development. It will make your activities even more powerful and relevant to all stakeholders if you document the outcomes of working in this way with children.

Questionnaires are a good way to gather evidence from children about their responses. Collating their written work in response to experiences will also show the impact of your provision.

Data from the SATs and internal assessments will also back up your reasons for giving children real, hands-on experiences. When I first came to West Rise, the Ofsted judgment I inherited was poor and the standards throughout the school in reading, writing and mathematics were very low. As the school has embraced a creative approach to teaching and learning, providing numerous opportunities for children to work outside, the results have improved dramatically. The school now has very good Ofsted judgments and excellent SATs results too. This is clear evidence of the success of this approach.

Remember that you need to show Ofsted the impact of your provision. As long as you can show that progress is being made, not just academically but also spiritually, morally and culturally, then they will be more than satisfied

Chapter 8

Preparing for Risk and Danger

Risk assessments

I often hear that people "cannot do activities because of the need to write a risk assessment". As you will see from the following explanation and example of a risk assessment, they are quite easy to create. Once you have written one, you will be used to writing others more effortlessly.

Writing a risk assessment can be pretty straightforward. It is also very important to do as it shows that you have considered all of the risks involved in your activity and have put in measures to prevent injury or death. No one wants a child or adult to be hurt as a result of your activities, so you must do everything you can to ensure that this will not happen.

Every risk assessment is unique and specific to the activity involved. Some activities which are duplicated still need to be reviewed however. An activity in fair weather will present different hazards to one which takes place during rain or snow. This is called an ongoing risk assessment.

When writing a risk assessment you need to think about why you are doing the activity in the first place. It needs to be worth doing to begin with to do it at all. Therefore, it is important to list the benefits, impact and purpose of the activity on your risk assessment.

Who is the visit leader and who are the adult helpers? Are they all competent?

For example, is the visit leader a qualified teacher and have they received the relevant and up-to-date training?

Within my school, the activity leader has to show me, as the headteacher, what their activity is. I then pass this on to the outside learning co-ordinator who will double-check it. By the time the activity has been declined or approved it has passed through several competent hands. This process however is by no means arduous. It will give you peace of mind in the end and confidence about the activity you are going to deliver. This way everyone can enjoy it and remain as safe from harm as is reasonably practical.

You will see from the example below that there is a section where you evaluate whether it is safe to do the activity. This is where you compare the level of risk to the likelihood of it happening. If there is a chance of serious injury or death, as in the example of teaching children paddle boarding or learning to shoot a gun, you need to evaluate whether your control measures are sufficient enough to prevent injury or death from occurring. If the likelihood is high, then you cannot do the activity. However, if the control measures are sufficient enough that the likelihood of serious injury or death is low then you may proceed.

With an ongoing risk assessment, which is an activity that is repeated, you cannot just use the same risk assessment. Firstly, you review what your control measures are; this is, in other words, what you are doing to prevent accidents from happening. Secondly, you must monitor how effective the control measures have been during previous sessions. This will be informed in part by the previous sessions but may also be influenced by changes to the environmental conditions, such as the weather. Finally, you must change, adapt and revise the risk assessment as required.

Please engage with your local Health and Safety Officer and where a generic pro forma is used by the school, as long as it has been approved by the Health and Safety Co-ordinator for the school, then use it. People in your school and organisation will most likely be used to using one particular format.

Ensure, as my staff do, that risk assessments are signed off correctly and that they have been seen by another qualified professional for errors and amendments.

It is also very important to make a site visit, if you are going off-site, before you take the children; if you are the trip leader then this is a requirement. Even if you are working on the school grounds, a site visit must be made. There could be broken glass in the area that was not there the day before. The weather conditions could have changed the level of risk involved so do not assume that the environmental conditions will always be the same.

Risk assessments are simply about taking full responsibility for the health and safety of everyone involved and ensuring as best you can that no one is hurt during your activities. They are not meant to be unnecessary or bureaucratic, it is part of the job and important to complete as accurately as possible.

Below is an example of a risk assessment from my school. The format may well be different within your school and we are continually updating our systems, so this is just a guide, although it will give you an idea of what is involved.

Risk Assessment

Establishment	Location		Date(s) valid
West Rise Junior School – Forest School	West Rise Marsh, Sevenoaks Road, Eastbourne		15th March 2016
Visit Leader	**Other Staff & Adults**	**No. Young People**	**Age(s) / Year Group(s)**
Helen Stringfellow	Mike Fairclough, Paul Hemmings, LM, PH, PW, SB (flint knapping)	24	Y5 9-10

Alternative Plan
If the weather is severe we will use the fire site situated at the front of The Studio on the school grounds.
When the fire site on the marsh is flooded, alternative areas will be used around the marsh.

Benefits / purpose
The children are taking part in a Bronze Age project. They will be learning about the Bronze Age, first hand. This will benefit the children because they will be learning about history and improving their Forest School skills, whilst having new experiences.
•   Raise self-esteem and self confidence
•   Team building and social skills
•   Connect with the natural environment locally
•   Promote independence and ability to manage risk
•   Bush craft skills

Emergency Contact Information and Procedure
Mobile phones will be fully charged and carried by Mike Fairclough, Helen Stringfellow (Forest School leader and first aider) and Paul Hemmings. Mobile phones to contact emergency services and the main school site.
There is a hard standing track leading from the road to the site where the activities will take place.

NOTE THE FOLLOWING

Ongoing risk assessment – the most essential element: 1. Apply the control measures 2. Monitor how effective they are 3. Change, adapt, revise as required

LIKELIHOOD		Low 1	Medium 2	High 3	Extreme 4
Unlikely / Rare	1	1 (Low)	2 (Low)	3 (Low)	4 (Medium)
Moderate	2	2 (Low)	4 (Medium)	6 (Medium)	8 (Medium)
Likely	3	3 (Low)	6 (Medium)	9 (High)	12 (High)
Almost certain	4	4 (Medium)	8 (Medium)	12 (High)	16 (High)

Section of Visit	Significant Hazards with Potential to cause harm	Control Measures	L	S	Risk Rating
Sites/ Environment/ Places Being Visits	Fall into lake or dyke.	First aider available (Qualification x 3 day first aid at work) Adult always aware of where children are in relation to boundary area. Water buoyancy aid available at all times. Spare clothing and footwear in safety bag. Out of bounds areas clearly defined Buoyancy aid and throw line to be accessible.	1	4	4
	Child wandering off and getting lost	Children always aware of where the group leader is to be found. Regular head count. Guidance given advice about not talking to strangers Supervising adult to be informed. Guidance given about petting unknown animals (remain calm do not wave arms with dogs).	1	3	4
	Adverse weather – electrical storms,	Obtain weather forecast and plan accordingly. Use school grounds if flooded or severe weather.	2	2	4
	Slips and trips on tree roots/ uneven steps/sticks etc.	Ensure activity takes place well away from rope lines such as those on tarps and shelters. Guidance for children on looking where they are going because of tree roots and slippery ground.	2	1	2
	Sickness (Toxicara) from dog fouling.	Site checked prior to activity for undesirables.	1	2	4
	Stings and scratches from brambles and nettles, plants.	Stop if children are not acting appropriately	2	1	2

81

Section of Visit	Significant Hazards with Potential to cause harm	Control Measures	L	S	Risk Rating
Sites/ Environment/ Places Being Visits	Poisonous toadstools/plants	Do not pick plants or fungi.	1	4	4
	Chased or attacked by the water buffalo bullocks	All livestock to be secured away in a paddock	1	4	4
		Don't let children walk ahead of adults on the marsh			
Activity Arrangements	Burns from the fire, cuts from tools – bowsaws, loppers, secateurs, fire strikers, knives, puncture wound from hand drill, potato peelers, and scalds from hot water – Kettle, fire spreading, burns from ignition of clothing or tinder.	Please also see attached individual risk assessments for the use of the following tools: bowsaws, hand drills, loppers and secateurs, knife /potato peeler, lighting a fire, cooking on a campfire and using Kelly Kettles.	1	4	4
	Child wandering off; Use of Forest School equipment unsupervised; Injury when transporting equipment around site; Injury during use of tools/equipment; Injury from breakage (tool, equipment); Burns/scalding from cooking; Injury or damage from fire spreading; Food poisoning; Food types & Allergic Reactions	FS Leader to give volunteers H & S briefing on safe use of tools, fire circle rules and site boundaries on arrival First aid always available. Carry mobile phone.			
	Cut a disc using a bow saw Use a hand drill to make a hole in the disc.	See attached risk assessment for tool use.			
	Sit around the fire.	Fire bucket and blanket to hand. Logs around the fire to stop spread.			
	Make a hot drink.	Clean drinking water taken.			
	Prepare and cook food over the fire.	Anti-bacterial soap for hands. Dietary implications – checked no food allergies. Discourage children from putting fingers in their mouths. Any cuts on hands must be kept covered with an adhesive plaster. Ensure all food is prepared and cooked properly.			

Section of Visit	Significant Hazards with Potential to cause harm	Control Measures	L	S	Risk Rating
Activity Arrangements	Use loppers and secateurs to cut low whips.	Guidance, support and demonstration given for using tools appropriately.	1	3	3
	Use a knife to remove bark. Use fire steels to light charcloth.	Clear instruction to be given (in demo and during use) Clear expectations of behaviour when using tools			
	Visiting the bee sanctuary	All children and adults to wear full protective bee suits including gloves and head gear with visor. To be accompanied by experienced beekeepers. Take small first aid kit with you.	1	4	4
	Burning from fire. One of the activities will be smelting – working a pair of bellows, which will be blowing onto a coal fire in the earth. Each child will have a go at working the bellows (with the help of a trained adult) and will be about 1.5 feet from the burning coals.	Safety talk prior to children being close to bellows and fire. Safety googles and gloves provided. Fire blanket and fire extinguisher close by. Trained staff operating fire equipment	1	3	3
	Flint knapping. The children will first observe an adult flint knapping. This is where a rock is hit against a piece of flint to produce a smaller piece of flint. Each child will then have a go at doing this.	Safety googles and gloves provided. Safety instructions given to children.	1	1	1
	Hand spinning – use a hand spindle to spin fleece. Germs from handling unwashed sheep fleece.	Demonstrate how to use a drop spindle. Wash hands after handling fleece.			
Transport	Walk to and from the marsh – Traffic on roads when crossing.	All adults to wear Hi Viz jackets to stop traffic. Children walk in pairs away from the road. An adult heads and tails the group. Head count on leaving and arrival to and from marsh.	1	4	4

Section of Visit	Significant Hazards with Potential to cause harm	Control Measures	L	S	Risk Rating
The Group	Not wearing the right clothing	All adults to check children have appropriate clothing and footwear for the weather. Spare clothing and footwear made available	1	3	3
	Getting distracted when using a tool	High adult to child ratio 1:4. No child given a tool unsupervised.			
	Not following instructions Running off.	Group to be counted at regular intervals. Work in small groups with a designated adult. Any vulnerable child to be made known to the adults.			
	Volunteers aware of Forest school safety procedures.	All adults to be given a copy of the Forest School Handbook, which includes all the health and safety procedures.			
	All adults to be briefed of any child's medical, health or behaviour issues where appropriate.	All adults to be briefed of any child's medical, health or behaviour issues where appropriate.			
	KH – asthma inhaler				
	FS List of children AR, JW, JF, LM, PD, EM, MW, EF, JB, AN, LW, FD JT (Needs asthma pump)				

Informing stakeholders

It is very important that your governors are informed and consulted about your activities or, if you work in an academy, that the strategic board are communicated with in the same way. There is a clear line of accountability and these people are at the top of the chain; it is also a good idea to keep them happy!

I recommend that you notify your Local Authority while it also really helps to engage with your Local Authority Health and Safety Officer. They will be able to advise you and to tell you where to find helpful and relevant documentation and policies. This will enable you to safely deliver all of your activities involving risk and danger. The more help that you can receive and the more transparent that you are, the better.

I have always held meetings with parents prior to certain activities, such as shooting when we first launch a dangerous project. My Forest School team also run an annual information evening for parents and there is an annual information event for paddle boarding. Parents who may be worried about possible health and safety risks will have their concerns addressed during these meetings. Parents need to be on your side and therefore you need their full permission for their children to engage in activities involving risk and danger.

It is important during these times to be fully prepared and to be able to answer all of the questions which may arise. If you have someone in the meeting who is against the idea you need to know what to say. So prepare very well in advance for these meetings and consider every question which may come up, as well as your comprehensive answers.

Schools also have insurances attached to them. It is vital that you, or someone on your team, contacts the insurance company and sends them copies of your risk assessments. This is particularly important if the activity involves significant risk or danger. My business manager, Sue Poore, has been excellent at contacting the insurance company which we use as a school. Sue has broached every subject with them, from purchasing water buffalo to using shotguns, teaching beekeeping and paddle boarding. There can be a lot of toing and froing between the school and the insurance company until everyone is happy but it is important to have these conversations. Make sure that there is a paper trail in the form of emails between key people as evidence that you have carried out all of your checks and procedures correctly.

I have found that most people and organisations think that activities involving risk and danger are an excellent way of providing children with a brilliant education. This is provided that the children and adults are kept safe and that everything is done to prevent any sort of injury. Individuals within the HSE or Ofsted, the local authority or the insurance company will often have a personal interest in the activity you are wishing to deliver. They may even ask whether they can join you when it happens.

Please also consult the HSE website and give them a call if you are considering something particularly dangerous. The HSE are there to help you, rather than to tell you not to do these activities, however no one wants anything to go wrong therefore it is vital that you prepare for your activity responsibly and correctly. This is to protect you, your staff, the children and anyone else you may come in to contact with during your activities.

Ideas for Teachers

Make a list of all the people and organisations which you are accountable to and let them know about your plans in writing. If you have people above you, do not do anything without their consent.

Make sure to enrol yourself on to a health and safety course. This might sound absolutely deadly but, if you are the headteacher, you are likely to also be the Health and Safety Co-ordinator. It is a legal requirement for you to be trained on a course and to be officially certificated. It is then your responsibility to inform your staff of the relevant procedures. You will more than likely to also find that the course is very interesting as well as very helpful.

If you are not the Health and Safety Co-ordinator then a staff meeting run by the Local Authority Health and Safety Officer will be able to help you. I strongly recommend schools to schedule a meeting specifically focused on writing a risk assessment, ensuring that this is revisited for any changes and for new staff on an annual basis.

Finally, once all of the risk assessments, insurances and plans are in place, hold a meeting with the parents and other relevant stakeholders to keep them informed and to answer any questions. With the parents on your side and with everything in place, you can enjoy the risky activities with your children knowing that you have done everything correctly.

Chapter 9

Love over Fear

My approach to education mirrors my approach to life. I have always felt very excited and positive about the world around me. I spend the majority of my spare time being creative in nature, having adventures with my wife and connecting with my children. I have built the philosophy of my school around this attitude.

It is an approach that resonates with children because they tend to engage with the world in exactly the same way as I do. I never grew out of this attitude to life and the past few years have taught me that plenty of other adults secretly never grew out of it either. Everyone wants to have enriching and exciting experiences and they want their children to have them too.

A powerful message to the education system

When West Rise Junior School won Primary School of the Year in 2015 I could never have predicted the extent to which it would open up opportunities for us. It raised the profile of the school astronomically. As described in this book, one of the people who took notice was Dame Judith Hackitt, then National Chair of the Health and Safety Executive (HSE). The very powerful message that she delivered to the education system and to parents was crystal clear. She said that coping with risk and danger is crucial to a child's education, it should become a key part of the school curriculum and that schools were currently "excessively risk-averse".

She told the nation's schools that children should be allowed to climb trees, play conkers, throw snowballs and embrace danger as an important part of their childhood. She also said that embracing risk and danger was preparing children for real life and adulthood. Dame Judith rightly highlighted how schools were failing children by being too risk-averse, she said that this would disadvantage children in the future and eventually leading to accidents in the workplace during later life.

West Rise received significant media attention, due to our collaboration with the HSE and the continued effects of receiving the TES award. Through television programmes such as BBC's *Countryfile*, BBC TV News and Channel 5 News, the message that children should be allowed to embrace risk and danger started to filter through to the general public. Many national newspapers also reported positively on the developments at the school, further advocating this approach within education to parents and colleagues across the entire country.

When presenter John Craven visited us at West Rise to film *Countryfile*, I told him about the fragments of clay pottery which Eastbourne Museum sometimes lend the school. As previously mentioned, these have the fingerprints of their Bronze Age makers visibly apparent within the material. John was very excited by this idea and asked me to contact the museum and ask to borrow them for filming. He felt that this would be very powerful for his viewers to see. He also felt that it was important for the viewers to see our work with the British Association of Shooting and Conservation (BASC).

Our collaboration with BASC has been very well supported in the past by Jon Severs, the Commissioning Editor at TES and a writer for the magazine. He had written a very balanced and comprehensive article about our work with BASC in the first year of our project. However, other journalists in the past had not been quite as supportive, so it was wonderful to have the backing of John Craven and the BBC at this time. The main point being that West Rise was being used as an example of how other schools could embrace working outside and that it has a positive impact on children's overall development.

So what's stopping us?

I have lost count of the number of teachers who have got in touch with me, following the press coverage, to ask about my methods or for a tour of the marsh on the back of the quad bike. They love what we are doing at West Rise and always bring new suggestions when they make contact with me. Through these connections I have realised that most teachers think in exactly the same way as I do. They just want their children to thrive, to be happy and to have amazing experiences. There seems to be a strong will within the profession and from parents to see this kind of positive change. So what is stopping this change from happening?

The late comedian Bill Hicks said that we always have a choice between fear and love. This is something which I firmly believe in as I feel strongly that we should not be limiting ourselves or the children in our care through fear. The reality is that headteachers and teachers are much freer than they often believe. Most importantly, we are also in the very privileged position to make a positive difference to children's lives whilst also having a lot of fun! However, we must stop focusing on our fears if we are to embrace this way of teaching and learning.

I find it very interesting that the list of educators from the past such as Badley and Steiner, through to contemporary thinkers such as Sir Ken Robinson and Bill Lucas, have all endorsed this way of working. Most educators, both past and present, believe that it is a worthy ideal to wish to provide children with exciting, hands-on experiences. Surely the time has come for every child in every school across the country to be given the education that they deserve and to stop blaming the system for that not happening.

The Late Victorian Education System, which Badley was surrounded by, included workhouses, corporal punishment and a hierarchical system which was impenetrable. Even within these extreme circumstances, Badley was able to have a vision for a more humane approach to education, which he eventually manifested and lives on to this day at Bedales School.

In this book, I have exposed some of the myths surrounding health and safety and Ofsted – both have previously been blamed as the reason why we are not able to take risks or to engage in dangerous activities with children. We have examined the important traits of grit and resilience, suggesting ways in which we can cultivate them. The essential ingredients for children and adults wishing to work in this way also includes being positive and aspirational. However, there has been a resistance from many schools to embrace these traits and to provide activities for their children involving risk and danger. This has been the product of fear, which we have all felt at certain times. This is as opposed to headteachers and teachers following their hearts and doing what they love and believe in. Unlike Victorian England, we are now in the perfect time and have the backing of the authorities to be able to embrace this way of working, if we truly wish to do so.

Trust and freedom

Another theme which has run throughout this book is the message that we need to cultivate trust and freedom within schools. The example of Room 13 shows how the ethos of this provision has permeated the fabric of my school on every level. Children need to be given opportunities to take up responsibilities and to be shown trust. We know that children are very sensitive, they can distinguish between real trust and a veneer of mistrust from the adults around them. Without real trust, there is no way that I would have felt comfortable about handing one of my children a shotgun or a knife or allowing them to light a fire.

There have been many times when a pupil has joined my school from another school with a contrasting culture and approach to trust and freedom. When these children first arrive, they need to be taught about the way that we do things at West Rise. Sometimes there has been a history of violence from the young person, so we put things in place to allow for the best possible chances of success. This includes a zero tolerance of swearing and fighting. If a child is heard to swear by an adult or is seen in a serious fight by an adult at my school, I will exclude them for a fixed period. The exclusion period is usually one day. I do this because everyone within the school, from adults to children deserve to be treated with respect and to feel safe and happy. The result being that I have sanctioned three official exclusions for one day in three years. This is considerably less than the average school. The child then returns to West Rise with a clean slate and positive behaviour targets.

The most powerful vehicle for the child's behaviour to be turned around is the loving culture we have grown at the school. Visitors comment on the relaxed and cheerful feeling around at West Rise. Children open doors for adults and exchange a please and thank you. Similarly, adults are respectful and kind to one another and everyone is treated as an individual. A very talented teacher at West Rise, Dr Andy McKechnie, turned the school into a "Unicef Rights Respecting School" a few years ago and also introduced "Philosophy for Children". These two initiatives are powerful vehicles for change and can be accessed online by any school wishing to improve the behaviour, self-esteem and self-awareness of their school community. The positive culture which radiates throughout West Rise is why troubled children at the school end up being happy, relaxed and non-violent. It is also the reason I can later hand them a rifle or a knife and know that I can trust them to use them safely.

Like most headteachers and teachers, I believe that schools should be happy and loving environments within which every child feels valued. They should not feel like harsh environments. This culture can only be created by the people within the schools themselves. Take everyone out of the school and it is just an empty building, so let's fill our schools with even more trust and freedom. This way children will be able to engage in activities involving risk and danger more safely and meaningfully.

Bridging the gap

A big part of my approach is rooted in bridging the gap between young people and the adults who care for them. I touched on this in the article about video gaming as a stimulus for working outside. Looking back over the decades and centuries, adults have always been complaining about children and young people. Totalbiscuit made reference to the medium of rock and heavy metal music, explaining that this sub-genre was massively misunderstood and misrepresented during the 1980s. I remember it well because I was part of that sub-culture myself as a teenager. I'm now a headteacher and still listen Rock music, but it does not appear to have done me any harm whatsoever!

The wedge which has now been driven between adults and young people because of their use of computers also needs to come to an end. If we are honest, where would we be if our kids were not showing us how to use our mobile phones and computer devices anyway? The trick is to find the link between their interests within the gaming world and activities within the physical world. Even more importantly, when children and adults bridge their perceived differences, they can then have better and more positive relationships with one another.

Taking full responsibility

I do not want to end the book without reiterating the need for good planning when embarking on activities which involve an element of risk and danger. Dame Judith Hackitt was not telling everyone to give their children knives and guns and then leave them to it. Her message, like the message in this book, has always been that we can expose our children to risk and danger as long as we are taking full responsibility for our activities. We are the adults in charge and children require us to be in that important role. This means adhering to health and safety regulations, writing risk assessments, communicating effectively with stakeholders and reviewing our systems on a regular basis. Of course this means doing our jobs conscientiously and will often involve hard but rewarding work.

Reiterating what I said earlier, it is highly recommended that you engage with your local Health and Safety Officer and the HSE. They will help you to make sure that you are doing activities with an element of risk and danger properly. This will prevent accidents from happening and will give you and your stakeholders peace of mind so that everyone can enjoy themselves.

Holding the vision

I began to formulate my vision for education over 20 years ago. It was inspired by my own childhood in which I freely roamed around the Chiltern Hills in

Buckinghamshire, taking my dad's air rifle out with me to go hunting. During my later years in North London as an art student, I experienced the benefits of creative freedom and the arts. Playing with ideas and pushing boundaries on every level of my being, West Rise Junior School has evolved organically and continues to do so as a result of these early influences on my thinking.

A fantastically positive team of educators, enthusiastic children, parents and supportive governors have allowed this vision to flourish over the years at West Rise. I attribute much of my positive outlook to my freedom-loving wife who has also encouraged me to work harder than ever and to step out of my own comfort zones, embracing the magic beyond. We are now expecting twins to be born next year, who like their brothers before them, will become pupils at my school wherever I may be. I love teaching, learning and believe passionately in embracing risk and danger as an integral part of my children's education.

What I would now love to see is more schools across the country offering their children the kinds of activities which Dame Judith and I have been advocating and which professionals and parents everywhere say that they want to deliver. In order to do this, schools must not get too distracted by creating a polarity between testing within schools and educating children in a creative way, including working outside. I believe that schools can do everything, including achieving highly in the SATs, if we are strategic about the way that we operate. The government and Ofsted are never going to ditch testing and inspections in favour of children working outside, but schools are in the unique position to integrate all of these important elements successfully.

I would also like to see the Governments rhetoric about resilience and character building profiled even more and schools supported in delivering on this agenda. Additionally, it would be very powerful if Ofsted were to have "Grit and Resilience" as a judgement category within inspections. This would encourage schools to find new ways to foster these qualities throughout the curriculum. Imagine in the future if schools could be judged to be outstanding in a category called "Risk and Danger".

However, rather than waiting for the government or Ofsted to tell us what to do, we can influence the shape of education ourselves by just getting on with it. There has never been a better time than now to do so.

Playing with Fire

"Playing with Fire" was conceived in response to hundreds of parents and professionals from across the country asking me, "so how do you get away with it?"

I hope that you can now see that I have not been getting away with anything at all. We have all had "permission" to embrace risk and danger within schools the whole time. I have underpinned the activities at my school with rigour in the form of systems and a philosophy for education which promotes trust and freedom. These underpinning elements are crucial to the success of such pursuits, however you do not need to do much at all to allow your children to play with conkers or to throw snowballs at each other. The kids have been doing that stuff for years. It is schools which need to change and not the system.

I remember a beautiful conversation I had with a child during our last "Spirit of the Marsh" experience at West Rise. I had just spent an hour pulling a trailer load of wood for the fire from the main school site to the roundhouse and then splitting the logs with an axe whilst a group of children were making the fire and erecting shelters. It was wet, windy and very muddy but already the children had a kettle of water boiling over the flames. Groups of children were foraging for food whilst others were busy flint knapping or tending the earth furnace with bellows. One particular child came over to me as I warmed myself against the fire and offered me a cup of hot coffee. He was covered head to toe in mud and had a small cut on his finger which he had received whilst flint knapping. He asked me how I was doing and then looked at me and said "this is the best day of my life". What more can anyone working with children ever wish to ask for than to hear that?

This is what motivates me to give children these kinds of experiences and why I invite you to do the same. Do what you believe in and embrace love over fear. Risk and danger are an important part of life and, as soon as you allow you and your children to fully embrace that world, you will see that this is where the magic happens and where real learning takes place. I hope that you will enjoy playing with fire.